A Teacher's Guide to
Standardized Reading Tests

Knowledge Is Power

Lucy Calkins

Kate Montgomery

Donna Santman

Teachers College Reading and Writing Project
Teachers College, Columbia University

with Beverly Falk

D0521804

HEINEMANN
Portsmouth, NH

Heinemann
A division of Reed Elsevier Inc.
361 Hanover Street
Portsmouth, NH 03801-3912
http://www.heinemann.com
Offices and agents throughout the world.

We would like to thank those who have given their permission to include material in this book.

CIP is on file with the Library of Congress
ISBN 0-325-00000-X

Editor: Lois Bridges
Production: Renée Le Verrier
Cover photographs: © Donnelly Marks Photography
Cover design: Darci Mehall, Aureo Design
Manufacturing: Louise Richardson

Printed in the United States of America on acid-free paper.
02 01 00   RRD   5

*To the brave and principled teachers everywhere
who struggle to teach according to their beliefs*

Contents

Acknowledgments

In many of the children's books that we love most, characters set off on journeys to faraway lands, to distant horizons. Often, their journeys are made easier by gifts. In *The Golden Compass*, Lyra is given a crystal ball that answers her questions. In *The Chronicles of Narnia*, Lucy is given a vial that heals wounds and restores vitality. We, too, have been given gifts. We've been given the greatest of gifts: the gift of mentors and companions.

Our thanks go first to Beverly Falk and her wise research associate, Suzanna Ort, who both joined our team, giving abundantly and generously of their knowledge and time. We are particularly thankful to them for having faith in us and in this book.

Our thanks go next to the extraordinary team from the Educational Testing Service, Ted Chittenden and Jacqueline Jones. Giants in the field of testing, they entered our study group as if they were our colleagues, taught by example, and joined us in the thrilling work of learning from teachers and children. From Jacqueline and Ted we learned, above all, how to learn.

Although it is customary to end one's acknowledgments with a nod to one's editor, we want to include Lois Bridges at the forefront of our statement, for she truly has been a mentor, helping us not only to write with courage and grace but also to consider the needs of the teachers who are our audience and to situate this work carefully into the fragile field of language arts education.

At home, in the Teachers College Reading and Writing Project, one person has stood out above all others: Kathleen Tolan's brilliance as a teacher and a thinker is woven into everything we say about test preparation, and we are more grateful to her than we can say. And, of course, this book would still be scattered papers and floating ideas if it weren't for the production wizardry of Jennifer D'Alvia.

We've learned alongside teachers and principals at P.S. 321 in Brooklyn, the Bronx New School, P.S. 11 in Manhattan, the Goose-hill Primary School in Cold Spring Harbor, and the Lakeside School in Merrick, Long Island. We are grateful to Lydia Bellino, Liz Phillips, Peter Heaney, Richard Goldstein, Dan Feigelson, Holly Kim, Esther Forrest, Brenda Steele, Kate Abell, Gloria Smith, and especially Claire Noonan and Katherine Bomer, whose ideas stud this book. We also want to thank Katherine for allowing us to photograph her beautiful classroom for the cover of this book.

Throughout the writing of this book, each of us has had special support. We would like to extend heartfelt thanks to Dave Hackenburg, Rae and Don Santman, and the members of the principals group within the Teachers College Reading and Writing Project community.

All of the work in this book stands on the shoulders of the Project's work in reading. This work has been made possible through generous funding from the Joseph E. Seagram and Sons Foundation. We are grateful to them.

Late in the process of writing this book, we realized we needed to lean on the expertise of wise educators from states whose assessment practices were different from those we know best. Susan Harman, Claudia Gentile, Sara Rudder, Angelle Batten, and Rene Essex joined us from the far corners of the nation, forming an intensive think tank on all the issues. Susan Harman deserves special mention, for she took on the enormous challenge of reading our early manuscript and giving detailed and lengthy responses. The manuscript was also read and reviewed by several others and we are grateful to them all. Monty Neil of Fair Test has been an especially generous and astute reader, and we thank him.

This book was brought through the process of copyediting and production at record-breaking speed because of Mike Gibbons' clarity, Lois Bridges' boundless energy, and Renée Le Verrier's hard work. We are impressed by the team Heinemann has assembled.

In *The Golden Compass, The Chronicles of Narnia,* and many other children's books, the characters travel to far horizons and in the end learn a new appreciation for home. We, too, reach the end of this journey with a new appreciation for home. We've thanked those who voyaged with us for a while, but we are most grateful to those who remain with us for life. How blessed we each feel for having had the chance to climb this high mountain with each other.

Author's Note

Although this book has been written by a team of us, we've chosen to write it in the first person. The "I" of this book, then, is fictional. There is no single person who has done all of this—developed a minilesson that likens the reading test to a scavenger hunt, worked with the staff of a private school to write a letter to parents about testing, interviewed ten-year-old Jared to understand his extraordinary success with tests, and other things.

The personal insights, metaphors, and memories of the "narrator" have been knitted together out of the yarns of several lives. Many of the teachers and children in the text are also composites.

LUCY CALKINS
KATE MONTGOMERY
DONNA SANTMAN

The Challenge

If you had told me a decade ago that I would be writing a book about standardized reading tests, I would have said, "Nonsense!" Standardized reading tests and I were official enemies. I'd spent my teaching career arguing that standardized reading tests don't measure what matters most about reading. They can't assess whether a child can use books as tools for finding information, for learning from other people and places, for working on projects, and especially for fulfilling dreams. Throughout my teaching career, I have worked hard to keep isolated reading passages and swarms of tiny questions from overtaking and controlling my teaching. I have clung to higher ground, fastening all my attention on the larger goals of helping children read and compose lives as powerful learners.

Then Tara Matthews was told she wouldn't get tenure as building principal unless her school's reading test scores went up. Tara! Tara, who hosted a breakfast study group for her staff on the teaching of reading each Wednesday morning all summer long. Tara, who drives between tag sales with a borrowed pickup truck looking for carpets and bookcases for her teachers. Tara, whose classes hold an average of thirty-six children.

Tara wasn't the only dedicated, progressive educator in jeopardy because of test scores, but she was the straw that broke this camel's back. Tara cannot afford to turn her back on the issue of preparing children to do better on standardized reading tests. Suddenly, neither could I. Nor could any of my colleagues from the Teachers College Reading and Writing Project. Across the country, standardized reading tests are assuming an increasingly powerful role in classrooms and schools. My colleagues and I could no longer turn away from the fact that we needed to do a better job of helping teachers and principals live under their shadow.

1

And so we formed a study group on standardized reading tests. Our group was composed of staff members from the Teachers College Reading and Writing Project as well as classroom teachers, principals, and reading specialists from Project schools. Two educational psychologists from Educational Testing Service (ETS)— Ted Chittenden, a leading researcher-psychologist and co-author of *Inquiry into Meaning,* a study of how children learn to read, and Jacqueline Jones, a research scientist, also with ETS and author of many articles on performance assessment, joined us as consultants and guided much of this work. We began researching in classrooms: observing students as they took simulated tests and documenting current methods of test preparation. Above all, we let the educators in our corner of the world know that we needed to understand the roles standardized reading tests were playing in their schools and classrooms.

I do not know why it took us so many years to hear the confusion, anger, and powerlessness that educators were feeling because of the high stakes attached to standardized reading tests. Suddenly we heard nothing else. Everywhere we turned, we heard stories of teachers who were being told, in the name of "raising standards," that they could no longer teach reading using the best of children's literature but instead must fill their classrooms and their days with worksheets, exercises, and drills. Too many desks were being pushed back into rows, and too many teachers were being pushed back into methods they didn't believe in.

We saw the impact of tests everywhere. In hamlets, towns, and cities across the country, newspapers rank schools. A school's ranking is usually determined only by its test scores. Schools are declared exemplary simply because the children in those schools achieve high test scores. No one looks more closely to see whether these children are avid, happy readers, whether book circulation in the school libraries is high, whether there is a culture of kindness, whether the classrooms are filled with thoughtful inquiry. Test scores alone are regarded as the measure of a school's quality— good or bad.

Not long ago, our local newspaper published a "dishonor roll" of schools. A school I know and love was on that list, a school where teachers arrive early and stay late, giving heart and soul to the challenge of teaching wisely and well. This is a school filled with children who have enormous needs but also with teachers who are going to the ends of the earth in an effort to meet those needs. It is a school so crowded that corners of the hallways have been turned into classrooms. The school library shelves have long since been boarded up, turning the library into yet another classroom. The teachers and the principal in this school need support, encouragement, and guidance in the uphill work of turning this school around. Instead, they are publicly humiliated.

Because of the high stakes associated with test scores, far too many educators across the nation are staffing their schools, grouping their children, and designing their curriculum with one goal in mind: to raise test scores. These schools particularly want to raise the high-stakes scores, the scores that "count the most."

I know of many schools in which the tests that count the most are given at the end of the third grade. It is not unusual in these schools for experienced teacher-leaders from the fifth and sixth grades to be moved into the third grade, the testing grade. The dislocated third-grade teachers, like it or not, are shuttled up to take the place of the anchor teachers in the upper grades. I also know of many, many schools in which children are referred to or detained in special education and bilingual classes simply so that they will not be in the testing pool.

Sadly, it is also true that sometimes the very children who need the most attention and who receive the lowest scores on the tests are ignored since their scores are nowhere near the level needed to make the school or district look good. When the only score that counts is the number of children scoring above the 50th percentile, reading specialists are often told to ignore children in the bottom quartile, focusing instead on children who score in the low middle range in hopes that their scores can be pushed above the 50th percentile, making the school or district statistics more impressive.

The emphasis on tests scores often pressures teachers to dumb down the curriculum. For example, teachers report that they ask for fewer essays because they believe essays are an inefficient means of preparing children for multiple-choice tests (Darling-Hammond & Wise, 1985; Shepard, 1989). When short-answer, multiple-choice tests are the only measure of student achievement, teachers are less apt to invest their energies in helping children conduct long-term, multifaceted projects involving independent research and writing. When the district's hopes are tied to bubbled answer sheets, teachers spend less time teaching children to conduct debates, work collaboratively, or pursue hands-on experimentation (Darling-Hammond, 1997).

The pressure to achieve high test scores often leads to curricular mandates that intrude on the professionalism and decision-making powers of teachers. In one large, urban school district, a district office testing expert dissected the previous year's reading test and identified ninety-eight discrete reading skills, including onomatopoeia, linking verbs, and compound words. Every school in the district was flooded with packets of ditto sheets on each of these ninety-eight skills. Every child of testing age received a separate packet of ditto sheets on each and every skill. The edict went out. Each child was to be taught, tested, and if necessary retaught in each skill area. No one questioned why an expert on testing (not on reading) had been given the power to design the reading curriculum for thousands of classrooms. No one asked whether what children truly needed was more drill on these decontextualized skills. Instead, the edict was clear: Every day, every district teacher was to teach one of the ninety-eight skills. The skill-of-the-day was to be displayed on chart paper on the wall of every classroom. District office staff members monitored this work with periodic surprise classroom spot checks during which they selected one child in each room to read aloud and define each skill on the chart.

In other schools across the country, test preparation work begins the first day of school and lasts all year. In some states, it almost seems to be state policy that every elementary school teacher begins his or her day by writing sentences filled with errors on the board and then asking the children to correct these sentences, just as if they were working on a standardized reading test. What a decision! Imagine that literally *thousands* of teachers fall into line, opening their school days with a drill on contractions and apostrophes. Why, I wonder, don't more people question whether this is the single most significant, inspirational, and rigorous way to call together our learning communities, to launch our days?

In one Midwest school district, it is policy that every teacher in the district be part of the effort to raise test scores. To ensure that this happens, the skills required to do well on the standardized tests have been analyzed and divvied up. Kindergarten teachers are expected to require daily practice in bubbling. Each morning, the little ones begin their day by filling in sentences such as

1. Today is _____.

- sunny
- cloudy
- windy
- snowy

Kindergartners (and struggling readers throughout all the grades) go by the name "bubble-children." Half in jest, a teacher from the district explained the label to me. "That's what we call the kids who can't do anything but bubble-in."

Last winter, the newspaper in one large city published a portrait of five schools that scored high on standardized reading tests. The article neglected to mention that almost every one of these schools had a competitive admissions policy, admitting only students who had already scored well on such tests. Instead, the article described the curriculum in each school as if to say, "If you, too, want high reading scores, follow these steps." One of the schools featured in the article was described as having "a Kaplan-like test preparation program" that begins in September and continues throughout the entire year. In another school, children all sit in desks arranged in rows, facing the chalkboard. This is true even in kindergarten classes. In this school there is no recess time, even for the youngest children. And these schools were portrayed as models!

For me, the hardest thing about these stories is that I know they didn't happen once upon a time, long, long ago, in a land far away. I know these are stories of today, here and now. And I know that I will not have answers. I cannot supply the good fairy who will enter into these stories, turning pumpkins into coaches, turning bad testing policies into good ones. I know there won't be a "happily ever after. . ." in this story. But I also know that sometimes what we need in life are the compromises we can live with, and the collegiality of knowing others are struggling alongside of us.

This project and this book have been a challenge for me and my colleagues in part because we do not have the solutions we wish we had. This has also been a challenge because we aren't experts on tests. Readers need to understand that this book is not written by world-renowned authorities on the topic of standardized reading tests but by a team of child-centered, progressive educators who have come to believe that in order to be less victimized by the tests, we need to become more knowledgeable about them. This is the story of our journey toward an understanding of standardized tests.

In the current educational climate, we—like Tara Matthews and many other teachers and educators—cannot afford to ignore assessment demands that seem alien to our educational philosophy and practice. But neither should we passively acquiesce, become apathetic, and let these demands take over our teaching.

We are concerned that, like us, other educators have been silenced and paralyzed by the high stakes attached to standardized reading test scores. I have seen too many teachers intimidated into allowing test-defined instruction to drive their schools toward a narrow definition of learning. I am concerned that the current national fixation on test scores has too often meant that control of the curriculum is being taken out of teachers' hands and put in the hands of district offices and publishers. This is an emergency, because we all know that learning and reading are enhanced by teachers who know their students and their curriculum well and who use their knowledge of children to diversify instruction to meet their students' needs.

There is a children's song that begins,

> Too high, can't get over it;
> Too low, can't get under it;
> Too wide, can't get 'round it . . .

and those words fit the current focus on large-scale reading assessments. My feeling is that we can't get over, under, or around the issue of tests. This book is intended to help us all get through it.

This book is truly meant to be a survival guide to standardized reading tests. We are particularly committed to helping progressive teachers live with standardized tests because we believe that these teachers face special challenges when it comes to preparing children for standardized, norm-referenced reading tests. We want to encourage all teachers, especially progressive teachers, to give careful attention to ways in which we can do wise and effective test preparation, for the following reasons:

- If our kids do not score high enough on reading tests, no matter what other evidence we may have of their growth in reading, we may lose the freedom to teach in the ways we believe are best for children. On the other hand, if our test scores are high, other educators will trust our teaching, and the best ways we know of teaching will spread to other classrooms.
- If our students do well on tests, we are in a far stronger position to be critical of those same tests. If we want people to listen to us when we say that an alternative means of assessment needs to replace or stand alongside tests, we will be heard better if our kids' scores are high. Politically, it is very awkward for a school district or a city to discard a test when large numbers of students aren't scoring well, because it looks as if teachers are giving up and turning to an easier form of assessment.
- In the short term, our kids get judged by these tests. No matter how invalid we may think the test scores are, a child's test scores can matter a great deal in the child's life. Test scores are used to track children, to identify children for remediation. Test scores can cause children to build identities as "smart" or "stupid."
- The ways with words some children have at home, the dialect of English they speak and the kind of talk they have, may be different from the language on standardized reading tests. If we don't introduce children to the genre and expectations of the tests, those who use language at home differently from the test will be at a disadvantage when trying to take it. Without an introduction to test language and format, children whose sociolinguistic groups are most different from that represented on the test will be much more likely to receive low scores.
- Taking standardized tests will be part of American life for the next few generations at least. Scores are often used for junior high, high school, college, and graduate school admissions, for

getting driver's licenses, for teaching and other civil service job certification, and for many other parts of life. Although each test is different, if we teach children ways to approach tests, the lessons can perhaps apply to many kinds of tests.

• If we make our methods of test preparation more potent, we can condense test preparation into short, powerful bursts at just the right times. We can feel more in control as a teacher, and there will be less risk that the test preparation will leak out all over the curriculum, spoiling everything.

We have written this book to help teachers live thoughtfully in the presence of tests and to do so without selling their souls. From the beginning, this project has been marked by concern that we might be selling our souls. Early on, our plan was to keep very quiet about our efforts to help Tara Matthews and the others live with standardized tests. We didn't want anyone outside of New York City to get wind of this work and to interpret our involvement as an endorsement of the tests. We joked about how it felt as if there were a sign hanging over the threshold of this project: "Abandon All Principles, All Ye Who Enter Here." The surprise is that we now feel *more* principled for having done this work.

Before I came to Teachers College, I used to teach in a small elementary school. Every Monday afternoon, the teachers and principal of our school would meet over potato chips and diet sodas, spending hours discussing school business and teaching methods. People had different views, but we gathered around a shared table. We disagreed on whether children should be divided into ability-based reading groups, whether desks should be in rows, whether every assignment should be graded. We disagreed about a lot, but there was harmony in our differences and we still ate lunch together. We still chatted about the details of our lives—about vacations, movies, families, and the news. I believed everyone around our table wanted the best for children.

In schools like mine across the nation, there are and have always been teachers who are more progressive and teachers who are more traditional. This can result in a wonderful learning community as long as teachers believe that we are in this work together.

Until recently most teachers in schools like mine did believe they were all in this work together.

But things change. Camps form. In some faculty rooms, it is as if a line has been drawn in the sand. Teachers whose children sit in rows eat at one end of the table, while the others cluster at the other end. Each group casts aspersions on the other. The traditional teachers complain, "My kids don't know *anything*. Someone has got to start teaching skills." At the opposite end of the table, progressive teachers complain, "My kids come to me *hating* reading." It is as if lasers are being shot across the table. No longer is there a sense of "We're in this together."

The camps are divided especially around people's responses to standardized reading tests. One group regards the tests as a necessary and honorable way to hold themselves and others accountable to rigor and standards. Any effort to side-step tests is seen as irresponsible and evasive. The other group feels disdainful of any preoccupation with test scores. "Standardized reading tests don't measure what matters most in reading," these people say. "Anyhow, the tests produce one-day, one-shot scores."

My colleagues and I watch all this happening, and we are concerned. When factions form, the conversations which yield so much stop. No one talks across the great divide, not about movies, books, or the weather, and certainly not about children, curriculum, and assessment.

We want to say, "Enough. Stop." It isn't going to work for colleagues to treat each other as enemies. We know from human history what happens when we "other" another person so that they become the enemy. We stop at nothing in our effort to annihilate them. After the Americans and the Japanese hostages were rescued from the Peruvian embassy, the newspaper headlines read, "All Freed—No One Hurt." No one hurt? What about the thirty-two Sendero Luminoso guards who were blown to pieces? Because these individuals were our enemies, we forgot that each one had a face, a story, a mother, a father.

In our schools, too, and in our national educational politics, sometimes it seems that people have coalesced into groups, declared each other to be enemies, and are now stopping at nothing. We are forgetting that each of our colleagues has a face, a story, a dream for children.

This isn't going to work. Someone has to cross the line in the sand, someone has to rebuild coalitions, and it might as well be me, it might as well be you.

No, I do not lose my principles when I move to the far end of the table, when I cross the line in the sand, when I say "You're onto something in your concern for the test scores. Can I join you in this?" I do not lose my principles when I say, "I was wrong to ignore the tests. I know that. But I'm not sure how to proceed."

I am also saying, of course, that I was wrong to ignore those who could see nothing but the tests. If we who teach and live in schools are going to regain a sense of common ground, we need to begin the dialogue. I hope this book encourages us to be ambassadors who cross the line in the sand, who pull up chairs alongside those who sit at the other end of the table. I hope this book helps readers to honor the intentions and take seriously the concerns of people who see things differently.

My colleagues and I have come to realize that we need to listen long and hard to voices we'd begun to ignore. And we've learned that we needn't fear that by taking on topics that are of major importance to others, we risk losing ourselves. After all, what principles matter more than those that revolve around listening, forming communities, having real dialogues, and being willing to outgrow ourselves?

In our work with New York City children, we often help youngsters from other countries to write their memoirs. Time and again, we see how their journeys have transformed the travelers, making them more self-conscious, more aware, and more clear about who they are. Because these children have lived in very different lands, they have a sense for the ongoing continuity of themselves.

We, too, have now traveled to a very different land. It's a land of stanines, reference groups, and distracter questions, yes, and it is also a land across the line in the sand. Rather than losing ourselves in this journey, we have instead become more self-aware, more reflective, and more clear about the ongoing continuities of who we are.

2

Learning Enough to Talk Back to the Tests

When my nephew was two, he planted a cornfield in his sandbox. Squatting alongside the homemade sandbox, Sam pushed his index finger deep into the wet sand, then dropped in a single kernel of popcorn, carefully covering it. Sam kept watch over his plot of soil, watering it with hopefulness. In time, tiny tips of greenery emerged, little rows of promise. Then Sam's family moved. As the moving men lugged the final items onto the van, Sam realized that no one planned to take his sandbox. Weeping, he cried, "Now I'll *never* see my seeds grow into a cornfield." Afterwards, I thought about how Sam's words captured the teacher's experience exactly. As teachers, we rarely get to see our kernels turn into cornfields.

Sometimes, just sometimes, there are moments when it feels as if someone spilled Miracle-Gro on a child, and we are blessed with the awesome privilege of watching a child sprout up before our eyes, visibly changing as a reader, a learner, a person. That was how it had been with Malik. He'd entered Anna's classroom at the start of fourth grade as an emergent reader, wobbling through books borrowed from the first-grade classroom across the hall, reciting words he'd learned by heart. As a staff developer in Anna's classroom, I returned weekly, and week by week, I watched Malik visibly progressing, until he was reading *Frog and Toad* with confidence, until he was well into the *Boxcar* series.

Anna and I couldn't wait for the results of Malik's reading test. We knew his scores still wouldn't be high, but we longed to see his proud progress registered in the rising incline of his score chart. Malik had scored only in the 18th percentile in third grade. Now, we waited happily for the new scores, for the concrete testimony to his hard work, to Anna's hard work, and to my hard work, too, as a staff developer.

Then the scores came. Randolph, Cheryl, Miguel, John . . . Malik. Malik? "Wait! It can't be." I whispered. There it was in black and white: Malik—18th percentile.

As teachers, all of us have had Maliks in our lives. We've all known what it is to be absolutely convinced that a child is making strong progress, only to hit a brick wall on test results. Malik: 18.

This year, my colleagues and I—the members of our test study group—turned the story of Malik into a cause. We resolved to figure out The Mystery of Malik. What could have gone wrong? How could Malik's tests have shown that he had made *no* progress?

The Mystery of Malik: Tests and the Struggling Reader

I don't recall what constellation of factors prompted me to climb a flight of stairs and walk down two hallways in search of Beverly Falk's expertise. Beverly is a colleague of ours at Teachers College. We are a reading-writing project, and she works at NCREST—the National Center for Restructuring Education, Schools and Teaching—where she directs an assessment project. We'd heard of Beverly's work, but our two worlds have always spun in different solar systems. It was Malik who led Beverly, my colleagues, and me to talk across the boundaries of our respective knowledge bases, our separate fields.

The first thing we learned was that Beverly wasn't so different from us after all. She'd been a teacher and a school principal. Her work with children, like our work with Malik, had led her to see most standardized tests as inadequate measures of what children can do, and to dream that perhaps she could make assessment systems that were more supportive of how kids learn. She created her own schoolwide assessment system and helped New York State develop a statewide language arts performance assessment for the early grades. To do this, she studied the history of testing, psychometrics, principles in measurement, and all the other stuff we'd avoided for so long.

For me, the main thing was that she'd studied Malik. She hadn't met my little guy, the one with the dark pool eyes and a sweet lilting voice that turned books into songs, but she had studied her own Maliks. And so I knew I wanted her as a tour guide through the rugged terrain of standardized tests.

"You are wrong to think his reading scores show no progress," Beverly said, and bit by bit I began to see. When Malik was in third grade, his 18th percentile score was established against the backdrop of his third-grade peers. He had to read considerably better in fourth grade in order to again earn an 18th percentile score against the new backdrop of older, more experienced readers. In fact, when children maintain their scores as Malik had done, one could say, "He has made one year's worth of progress." Then, too, the true story behind Malik's scores was complicated by the fact that the scores had been reported as percentiles rather than as raw scores. His *raw* scores might have gone up (or down); it was his *percentile* score that remained at 18. This percentile score does not reflect the number of questions Malik got right or wrong on the exam. It represents the percentage of children in his "norming group" who did worse than he did. Thinking about it, I realized that on a pediatrician's height chart a child who had grown three inches in a year could still receive a lower percentile score, depending on whether most other children of the same age had gone through a greater growth spurt than he had during that year.

Sighing a bit with relief, I said, "So, it *is* true that his reading got better!"

Beverly looked at me, her eyes widening. "You amaze me," she said. "You came here full of detailed stories about Malik's progress as a reader. You've seen that progress with your own eyes. Yet, until I showed you that the test scores show growth, you were ready to disbelieve all you've seen. Why do you think a test knows more than you know?"

I knew Beverly was right. Debbie Meier, the famous principal of the Central Park East school, who was awarded a MacArthur Fellowship for her educational leadership, once made a similar point. She commented that when people trust test scores more than their first-hand experience, it is rather like a person standing in the midst of a swirling snowstorm, saying, "I need to call the weatherman to see if it's snowing" (Meier, 1991).

Later in this book, I return to the issue of helping teachers trust their own findings about children like Malik. I suggest that perhaps in order for teachers like us to use our informal assessments as a North Star, in order for us to trust our homespun methods of assessment, we may need to be a bit more systematic and formal in our classroom-based observations. Perhaps we also need to systematically document growth along prechosen then-until-now continua.

It was a consolation to learn that just because Malik had scored in the 18th percentile in both the third and the fourth grades, his scores didn't suggest that his reading level had stayed in one place. But my mind and soul still rebelled against the dirt-lowness of his scores. Beverly was right: I'd seen his growth as a reader with my own eyes. I knew enough to be certain that at least his newest 18th percentile score was a miserably flawed reflection of Malik as a reader.

"You're right about Malik," Beverly said, anticipating what I was thinking. "These tests don't do a good job of showing what kids (and especially struggling kids) can do as readers." Together we began to consider the limitations of tests for children like Malik.

One thing that stood out was the role that interest played in Malik's ability to demonstrate his skills. He especially loved books about cats. Because he often fed the cats that lived behind his apartment building, books on cats resonated for him. He brought his own images, stories, and associations to their pages. On the reading test, he'd been asked to read a slew of separate passages, each unrelated to the next. One was on the architecture of sixteenth-century English churches, another was on the chemistry of filmstrip development. Malik had little interest in either of these topics, nor did he care much about the other topics he encountered helter-skelter on the other pages of the test. And in his entire life Malik had almost never been asked to read in this way—a hodgepodge of passages, each on a completely different topic. The entire experience of reading the test was utterly unlike the reading he had begun to do with such emerging competence in his classroom.

To make matters worse, in order to get the gist of the passages, Malik needed background knowledge in many things that were utterly foreign to him. So-called reading tests are often assessments of background knowledge more than tests of reading. Because of this, these tests often disadvantage children from poor or culturally diverse backgrounds, (Edelsky, 1991; Fair Test; Meier, 1991; Webster, McInnis, & Crover, 1986). Beverly told me about

Josue Gonzalez, one of our colleagues at Teachers College, who recalled a reading test he had taken as a child growing up in a small town in New Mexico. One of the passages on the test was about maple trees, something Josue had never seen in the desert area where he grew up. Josue had difficulty answering the questions, not because he couldn't read the words, but because he had no idea what the content of the passage was about.

Malik was in the same position as Josue. He wasn't familiar with the terminology of time: centuries, decades, and the like. He didn't know much about England and didn't realize that Great Britain and England were almost synonymous. He'd never learned about film being developed in a darkroom. In fact, he'd never held a camera, never adjusted the focus of a camera lens, never watched a homemade video. For Malik, the "general knowledge" requirements on the reading tests were particularly debilitating because Malik's teachers, like so many others across the country, are so concerned with their children's reading, writing, and mathematics skills that other disciplines have been squeezed out of the school day. Malik spends his entire morning in school on reading and writing, and he works on social studies or science topics only three times a week for thirty minutes. Is it any surprise that he can't place Great Britain on his mental map? Across town, other fourth graders take the same test that Malik takes. Most of these children have cameras of their own. Many have parents who have traveled to England and shelves of books on other countries. Malik does have knowledge about lots of things: give him something to read about cats or fish or the New York City subway system, his latest passion, and you'll see a different reader than the reader he was on this particular test. His interests and knowledge base simply did not match the knowledge base required to negotiate this test.

The makers of tests sometimes do try to avoid passages that privilege certain children over others. When Beverly was developing prototypes of a new test for New York State, she figured that hurricanes might be a reasonable topic and only later realized that the topic of hurricanes privileges kids from Long Island, who have lived through more hurricanes than they want to remember. The topic of hurricanes would be less familiar to children from communities in western New York. Despite some test makers' efforts to find topics that are not geographically, culturally, or linguistically biased, the fact remains that Malik's knowledge base is not well-suited to standardized tests. Debbie Meier questioned whether reading tests assess general knowledge more than they assess reading. Meier (1991) points out that sometimes when children answer questions incorrectly, it is not because of a reading problem but because the children's knowledge or sense of logic differs from that of the test writer. One test Meier described contained this question:

An architect's most important tools are _____.

    E   pencil and paper
    F   buildings
    G   ideas
    H   bricks

Many children selected "(E) pencil and paper," which, according to the score sheet, was incorrect. According to the test writer, the correct answer is "(G) ideas." Did these children have reading problems, or was it something else entirely? Meier also described this question:

A giant is always _____.

    E   huge
    F   fierce
    G   mean
    H   scary

The correct answer is "huge," but many children answered "scary." Does this mean that these children have problems reading, or does it mean that for them giants are scary?

Meier goes on to point out other instances where obtaining the correct answers on a reading test "required knowing that . . . a tree trunk has 'rings' inside (and not the kind you wear on your finger); that oceans have tides (and that they go in and out every twelve hours); that penicillin is a drug; that 1865 is one hundred years before 1965—and other facts that are unlikely material for a sound second-grade curriculum (unless the teacher has peeked at the test ahead of time)!" (1991, pp. 458–459). Of course, it is important for children to build as wide a knowledge base as possible, but it is also important that we assess their ability to read, separately from their background knowledge. The irony is that as long as our classrooms continue to focus narrowly on raising test scores, it is unlikely they will provide the rich, comprehensive reading program that can provide children with this wide range of knowledge.

When reading tests assess a student's knowledge, there is often a risk of bias because the content that test makers expect all children to know will usually be content that is especially prevalent in the lives of middle-class children. And test bias is not limited to the *content* of the passages. As we looked over sample test questions from a variety of nationally used standardized tests, we found questions on grammar and language use that present extra challenges for children who come from culturally and linguistically diverse backgrounds. Often the questions offered response options that were wrong but could seem correct to children whose first language was not standard English. For example, in one question, the readers were asked "Which of the following sounds best?" The listed alternatives included "You *needs* to put the wood on the fire" and "You *need* to put the wood on the fire." To Malik, the incorrect answer *sounded* right because it was similar to the language used in his home. To choose the right answer he could not rely simply on what *sounded* best or what came to him intuitively. For Malik to provide what the test makers regard as the correct answer, he would need to code-switch, to think about what would sound right to the test maker.

These subtle and not-so-subtle socioeconomic, cultural, and linguistic biases affect test scores not only for Malik but for all the students in our nation. Socioeconomic and racial/ethnic backgrounds are highly correlated with test performance. For example, on the National Assessment of Educational Progress (a nationwide exam developed three decades ago to keep track of national trends in student learning) 70 percent of fourth graders whose parents graduated from college and 71 percent of *white* fourth graders received scores showing that they were reading at or above what the test regarded as the *basic* level in reading. Only 31 percent of African-Americans, 35 percent of Latino and Latina students, and 35 percent of children of high school dropouts scored as well (Slavin, 1997).

I also came to understand why these tests aren't the most sensitive measures of a struggling reader's progress. If *I'd* wanted to understand Malik's proficiencies as a reader and to compare him to other struggling-but-progressing readers in my classroom, I wouldn't normally do this by having these children read passages that were far beyond their instructional reading levels. Instead, I would have asked Malik to read something that felt like a right fit. In standardized tests, rather than seeing what Malik can do while working at his level, I see what he can do with texts that are way too hard for him. I would have learned more by seeing his skills for coping with the Boxcar series.

By this time in my course of study, it had become pretty clear to me why Malik hadn't scored higher on the test. But there are other reasons, which relate to poor test takers the world over. In every classroom there are some children who are avid, strong, thoughtful readers, and yet they do not receive standardized test scores that indicate this. The multiple-choice format of tests is a big obstacle for many of these children. One problem is that test writers include so-called distracter responses, and these do indeed distract. For example, questions will be followed by answers that are partly right or that *could* be right if looked at in a particular way.

Also, some of the optional answers for multiple-choice questions *could* be regarded as true if readers draw on information that they might know from experience. Because this information is not in the reading passage that precedes them, however, readers get penalized for selecting these answers. A well-known example was given in Miriam Cohen's *First Grade Takes a Test* (1980). This is the story of a young child's first reading test. The child reads a passage about rabbits and then comes to a question about the kind of food rabbits like to eat. According to only the information supplied in the reading passage, the correct answer would have been "lettuce." In Cohen's book, the young heroine had been feeding the rabbits in her classroom all year and was convinced that their food of choice was carrots. After skimming the listed options, she saw that "carrots" wasn't included as a possibility, and so she took up her pencil and added "carrots" beside the bubbles on her answer sheet. Of course, she got that question wrong. Yet she had been able to read the passage perfectly. In our everyday reading lives, indeed in our learning lives, we draw on all that we know in order to make sense of texts and experiences. Good teachers regularly encourage children to do this. Only when taking such tests are children required to go counter to their normal practice of constructing meaning by drawing on outside knowledge.

Sometimes it's children's own experiences that lead them away from correct answers, as in the previous example. But at other times it's their knowledge of the world of reading and writing that misguides them. One test passage told the story of two girls whose parents had gone on vacation. The girls let the house get dirtier and dirtier until they finally had to clean it up quickly before their parents returned home. In choosing what would make "a good title for this passage" one student incorrectly chose "Rotting Meat" instead of "Cleaning the House." The child explained her choice by saying that "Cleaning the House" would be too plain. "Rotting Meat" would make readers curious, a criterion for a good title that she had learned in her writing workshop. "And anyhow, the girls *were* spoiled," she said, "so they were, in a way, *rotting.*"

Sometimes when we, as adults, look at the tests our children are asked to take, it's hard for us to imagine why test makers regard some answers as right and others as wrong. For example, one practice test contained a poem about a woman who had twelve children and lost eight of them, who worked keeping her home and making her garden, and who shouted to the hills and sang to the valleys. One of the test questions was "The narrator feels her life was (A) filled with unhappiness, (B) too short, (C) a very full life, (D) very dull and boring." The child I observed was stymied because two answers seemed true. Although the correct answer was "(C) a very full life," in the end she decided the old woman's life was "filled with unhappiness," because, she said, "How could you lose eight children and ever feel happy again?"

Another way that multiple-choice questions confuse some children is by offering options that are only partly true. For example, if a question asks "Which of these is the main idea of the story?" one of the possible answers is apt to be an item that is, in fact, true, but not the main part of the story. Some children will inevitably choose this answer because they recognize it as a true part of the story.

Already, I had learned more about tests than I had ever wanted to know (until now). I could now talk about test bias, correlations between tests and income, and some of the differences between tests of reading and real reading. I began to feel that I knew some things that could help children and parents stop regarding a child's reading test scores as an all-important verdict. But it wasn't enough.

As my colleagues and I met around the big table in our office, we realized that we had been unbelievably naive about tests, and that the teachers and principals with whom we worked were this way as well. We were thankful that Beverly Falk, Ted Chittenden, and Jacqueline Jones were helping us think about these tests, but we wanted even more help. We resolved to learn from teachers and test experts across the country, both through conversations with them and through the distant membership of reading their articles and books (Edelsky, 1991; Goodman, 1992).

In honor of my new inquiry, I had bought myself a spiral notebook and written "Know Thy Enemy: A Study of Standardized Tests" on the title page, just as if I were a graduate student. When I showed my spiral notebook to Beverly, I laughed about how weird it felt for me to actually be excited about a study of tests. Beverly pointed to my title page and said, "You've got to revise the title, you know. Standardized tests aren't necessarily the enemy. The enemy is tests that don't represent the best of what we know about children as readers. The biggest problem is that tests are *norm-referenced*."

My bubble of excitement collapsed. I felt deflated. All these terms drove me nuts. What was she saying? What was the difference? I knew a bit about norms, of course, but I didn't have a clue about the difference between "standardized" and "norm-referenced" tests. I felt stupid.

Understanding the Lingo

Now I look back on that day's lesson and realize that it was fundamental for me to learn to distinguish between the terms *standardized* and *norm-referenced*. What the term *standardized* means in relation to a test is that people are measured in a uniform way. We give one exam to everyone under exactly the same conditions. Everyone takes the test on a given day, hears the same directions, reads the same passages, and has the same amount of time to complete the test. Standardized tests are used to measure pupil progress, and many people regard them as necessary to provide information as to ensure that a fair and equitable education is offered to every child. The logic behind this is as follows. Suppose two third-grade children from different communities were each given an A in reading. What evidence do we have that the programs they experienced were teaching the children similar things or that the A in one place meant the same as the A in another place? These questions are the rationale many people give for using standardized reading tests. Some people believe that it is especially important in our country to have a standardized way to measure the education all children receive because our culture has deeply ingrained biases against people from some ethnic and socioeconomic groups, leading these people to receive fewer opportunities than others. Our biases even lead some people (even some educators) to have lower expectations for children from some racial and economic groups. Keeping track of all children's progress on the same standardized tests can be a way to challenge everyone to treat all children in similar ways so that all children have the opportunity to achieve similar standards. This, then, explains why it's not right for me to title my notebook, "Know Thy Enemy: A Study of Standardized Tests."

It is important to note, however, that there are nevertheless problems and tensions around the issue of standardization. One problem is that it isn't easy to standardize measurement of a complex thing such as reading. It is especially difficult to find cost-efficient, timely, and standardized ways to measure reading across large groups of children. In order to do this, tests of reading tend to involve paper-and-pencil multiple-choice questions, and in such tests children are asked to do very different things than they do as readers in their daily lives. That is, our effort to assess reading can lead us to assess something that is not reading.

I have come to realize, however, that the fact that some people want a standardized measure of children's abilities as readers doesn't mean that we must turn reading into something that is not reading. To be standardized, a test need not have multiple-choice questions, lots of little passages, or places for bubbled-in answers. A standardized test could require children to read a book aloud with 95 percent accuracy and then retell the story. One way to standardize such a test would be to have the books be equally unfamiliar (or familiar) to all children. There would need to be an efficient way to translate the retelling into scores and probably for someone other than the classroom teacher to administer and score the test. Raters would need to work under clear guidelines so that one rater's scores would be apt to match another rater's scores. This would give the test what is called inter-rater reliability.

In high-stakes situations, people may question whether such a test is "technically strong." For example, Kentucky is famous for having one of the best performance-based exams (Jones & Whitford, 1997). In Kentucky, children write extended responses to the readings. Recently, however, perhaps because of the high stakes attached to this test (teachers get extra stipends when their children's scores move up), people have begun to fret over how objectively the tests are scored. They are concerned that the sanctions and rewards attached to results are influencing test raters' judgments as they read and score open-ended student responses. In a way, one could say that the more a test allows for extended response or for choice, the more difficult it is to ensure that the test is technically strong. There are trade-offs in the world of assessment. When high stakes are attached to tests, and the tests are open-ended, it is more likely that the tests will be critiqued over the issue of technical standards. To avoid such problems, sometimes extended-answer questions end up being turned into multiple-choice questions. The problem, then, is that when there are important consequences to students' scores, there is added pressure to make tests technically stronger, which often results in tests that do not assess real reading. The term for how well a test measures what it purports to measure is *construct validity*. Sadly, most tests of reading are sorely limited in this regard.

There is another problem that comes with standardizing tests. It is ironic that our nation is obsessed with developing standardized ways to measure children's progress as readers when their opportunities to learn are in no way standardized. Before we can draw any conclusions based on children's performances on standardized reading tests (that is, before we blame the teachers, the curriculum, or the kids), we need to recognize that we do not have an even playing field.

Imagine that there was going to be a giant race between all the children of the nation. Everything in this race is to be kept absolutely equal because the stakes are so high. To ensure that this happens, microscopes focus on the starting line. No one's toe may cross the line by even a minuscule amount. Everyone's shirt must weigh exactly the same. Everyone begins the race with exactly two sips of water. But, meanwhile, no one notices that half the children start the race at a starting line five miles back from the line where the others start the race. "On your mark, get set, go!" The children are off. Some children run faster than others and still don't come close to crossing the finish line first. The children who are the winners are not necessarily the fastest. Instead, the winners are the children who got the head start.

I was fairly clear by now why standardized tests weren't necessarily the enemy, but I wasn't certain what the difference was between standardized and norm-referenced tests. I still wasn't sure why Beverly had told me to rename my notebook "Know Thy Enemy: A Study of Norm-Referenced Tests." Now I forgive myself for not understanding the differences at the time, because I now see that most standardized tests are also norm-referenced. But I also see that it is when they are designed to be norm-referenced that standardized tests become particularly problematic.

When a test is norm-referenced, it is developed to demonstrate how a student compares with other students. That might seem reasonable. What's wrong with parents, teachers, administrators, and students wanting to know how the students measure up against others across the country? After all, as Robert Rothman points out in his book *Measuring Up: Standards, Assessment, and School Reform* (1995), without norms for comparison, the statement "He is six feet tall and weighs one hundred pounds" would be meaningless. Only our knowledge of what the average weight might be for someone who is six feet tall can lead us to conclude, "He is thin."

But norm referencing presents several problems, stemming from how the actual items on the test are developed. Let me try to explain. Norm-referenced tests are designed to produce scores that fall on a bell curve. To achieve this, items considered for placement on the test are pretested on a sample of students that is supposedly representative of our nation's demographics. As a result of this pretesting, a set of items is chosen that contains only a *few* questions that *most* students will able to answer. The bulk of the items placed on the test are ones that only some, but not many, of the students can answer. The problem with this is that the test development process is guided by the attempt to sort and rank students in relation to each other. It is not guided by an effort to reflect what students actually know and can do. As Clifford Hill has written, "Indeed, if a particular question doesn't sufficiently discriminate among people during its trial run, it doesn't even get included in the test. . . . Test passages are often deliberately restructured so that they can accommodate questions that will discriminate among test-takers" (1992, 11). In other words, if too many students do well on a pretested item, regardless of the importance of its content, the item may conceivably be left out of the final version of the test so that the test will produce the necessary bell curve of performance.

Ted Chittenden once explained norm-referenced tests with the following example. Imagine that a test is being designed to rank five flutists, all of whom have been studying for a year and each of whom is roughly equivalent to the others in overall ability. The test, in its quest to determine who is "the best," would have to contain exercises that bring out the *differences* among the five flutists. For example, one strategy might be to note the time it took each player to complete a piece. If this factor were used as the discriminator, then while all the players might be equally able to perform the piece, the one who played it the fastest would be ranked first. Other important qualities of playing, especially those that are more difficult to measure, such as depth of expression, would probably *not* be included on the test. So the flute player that brought tears to the eyes of her listeners because of her sensitive phrasing and nuancing would not be credited for this skill. She might well be overlooked in favor of a player who could play the piece faster.

Some of the testing experts with whom I worked gave a similar example for the Scholastic Aptitude Test (SAT). It is common knowledge among test makers that there is not a significant statistical difference between, for example, a score of 630 and a score of 590 on the SAT. That is, if a student, for example, earns a score of 630 one day and then retakes the test the next day, that same student might well receive 590. Another way of saying this is that the difference between the scores of two students, one who received 630 and one who received 590, could be accidental. Ted and other testing experts at ETS advocate reporting scores in bands (see Chapter 10) and not as the precise scores of individuals. But, of course, reporting students' scores in bands doesn't always satisfy those who especially want to be able to sort and differentiate individuals. The purpose of norm-referenced tests is to differentiate between individuals, and to do so even when people are, in fact, roughly equivalent.

The criterion-referenced test is different from a norm-referenced test. The best example of a criterion-referenced test is the Department of Motor Vehicles' driving test. In this test, there are clear, publicly articulated standards, derived from what a community determines is necessary for all drivers to know in order to have safe streets. The standards are delineated publicly and clearly so that everyone can prepare to meet them, and we all hope that everyone will master the standards and pass the test.

The goal of a norm-referenced test is to make it impossible for everyone to pass. And the criteria for doing well on norm-referenced tests are usually kept secret for "security purposes." Even after these tests are completed, teachers, students, and parents often don't see the tests again, and they are therefore not able to learn from an analysis of correct and incorrect answers. The secrecy accompanying norm-referenced tests exists in part because the goal is to divide people who do well on these tests from the people who don't. In fact, norm-referenced tests are designed so that 50 percent of the national sample of test takers score below the midpoint, which is defined as grade-level. Of course, any one individual or any one local community can work hard and come out ahead of the national norms. However, if too many communities succeed in doing this nationally, the test will be redesigned with more difficult questions or it will be renormed so that, regardless of how proficient students might become, half of them will still fall below the midpoint (Cannell, 1987, 1989).

Beverly explained to me that this way of using norm-referenced tests to sort and rank people has a long history, dating back to the early part of the twentieth century when as a nation we became enamored of science and the belief that scientific and objective ways could be found to measure the capacities of different individuals and to predict their future possibilities. From the beginning, the process was flawed because the "objectivity" was subject to the fluctuating biases of the times. For example, when intelligence tests were first being developed, women outperformed men. This discrepancy was unacceptable, given the era's attitudes about women's inferiority. So the tests were adjusted until men excelled in acceptable proportions (Darling-Hammond, 1994). A similar process happened at other points in our nation's history when tests were used to determine who would have access to limited opportunities for schooling or jobs. When the performance of certain immigrant groups was jeopardizing the dominant culture's access to these opportunities, the tests were redesigned to ensure that the appropriate people (according to the views of the time) got the sought-after openings (Hanson, 1993).

The good news is that a new kind of standardized test is being developed that addresses some of the problems of norm-referenced standardized tests. This kind of test does not determine how well students perform by comparing one against the next but instead assesses what students know and can do in relation to publicly articulated standards that have been commonly agreed upon. These so-called standards-based tests are also criterion-referenced tests, like the Advanced Placement exams. Everyone is able to know ahead of time exactly what knowledge and skills are expected, and everyone can work to meet these public standards. If we work hard, and if we all have the resources and supports we need (this is critically important), all children should stand a chance of meeting the standards, of passing standards-based tests.

The New Standards tests are a good example of criterion-referenced tests. Their criteria reflect standards that have been set by the national organizations, such as the National Council of Teachers of English. These and other standards-based tests often aim to measure what students know and can do through a variety of performances rather than by relying solely on the paper-and-pencil format. While it is harder to standardize performance-based demonstrations of knowledge and skills, it is possible to do so. For example, Beverly and other teachers in New York State have developed a performance-oriented, standards-based standardized way to assess reading for the early grades. One part of it requires children to read a text aloud and then retell it to the teacher. The test is standardized in that it asks all teachers to keep track of the same kinds of skills and strategies that their students use during the "performance." This information is evaluated in relation to a reading scale that contains descriptions of reading behaviors at different stages of development.

The catch-22 of these new efforts is that one of the ways that new forms of tests are validated is by comparing their results to those of existing tests. For example, sometimes even when a whole new test has been developed with the goal of better assessing reading achievement, the test makers still must demonstrate their test's worthiness by showing that children who answered 18 percent of the answers right on the new test achieved a similar score on existing tests. The new test is then said to correlate with preexisting tests, meaning that the same children have scored similarly on both tests. The validity of tests that produce scores straying too much from this "natural order" is sometimes questioned. This, of course, acts as a conservative force in the world of testing, anchoring new, improved tests to older tests.

Questions to Ask

By this time, my head was spinning with testing lingo. My study group and I decided that the only way to feel at home with this new information was to begin using our new testing vocabulary and our new ideas. We made a point to try to speak often about tests. We'd speak eruditely about norm-referencing groups, the schedules for renorming tests, predictive validity, and so forth, feeling very much like my third graders must have felt when they were asked to incorporate new vocabulary lists into their everyday speech. But it worked. The more we used the testing terms and concepts, the more questions we had to bring back to Beverly, Ted, and Jacqueline, and to the reading we were doing. Bit by bit, we began to see ourselves becoming more thoughtful consumers of tests.

I now know that if I were hired to teach in a new district, I'd have lots of questions to ask about the tests given in that district. My first question would be whether the test was norm-referenced. I'd *hope* the answer would be that it was a criterion-referenced test. This would suggest to me that there were clear criteria for success on the test and that the goal was for children to do well on it. My hope would also be that the test had a high level of construct validity, that is, that the requirements for doing well on the reading test closely matched the requirements for being a good reader in life.

After considering whether the test was norm-referenced or not, and thinking through the details of this, I'd also want to ask whether the test was standards-based. In forty-nine out of the fifty states, the direction of assessment has been to make it standards-based, which means that states are trying to evaluate kids' progress toward explicit standards. Although each state has developed its own package of standards, as one looks across states it is clear that the standards from state to state are quite consistent with each other (*Education Week*, 1997).

It has been clearly crucial for test-publishing companies to follow the lead of the states. Many states bring together groups of educators to develop and pilot standardized assessment systems based on their own language arts standards. After all the work done by the team, however, the states sometimes turn to a "big vendor," a national publisher of basals and tests, to bring the pilot to scale and to include nationally normed questions so that children from state to state can be ranked against children nationally. The companies that publish national tests offer to customize their tests to meet the supposedly unique standards of each particular state. These states then claim to offer their own customized standards-based test. In a number of states that have *not* worried about producing national norms, people have been agitating for their state tests to be revised so that parents can learn how their children compare with children from all over the country. As a result, more and more states are taking their tests to publishers and saying, "Create a nationally normed test that reflects our own state standards and that contains questions from our state's pilot test."

One could argue that although the resulting tests are described as customized and standards-based, in truth the new tests are in many ways similar to the old ones—only in a new disguise. Susan Harman, a teacher-researcher at Cleveland Elementary School in San Francisco, for example, found that fully 46 percent of the items on a "new" California Frameworks Assessment were also on the old California Test of Basic Skills (Harman, 1996). Still other items were remarkably similar. This example illustrates how the process of "customizing" can be much like a librarian's choosing from a stock of old books to create a new display on, say, contemporary literature. In theory, when publishers are hired to create new tests based on the specific needs of a particular state or district, they should not just pull old questions off the shelf, assemble them, and call it a day, but some of this does happen, because of an emphasis on norm referencing and keeping costs down. It is very expensive and complicated to create an entirely new normed test, because one has to create a whole new norming process. Therefore, according to publishers, using old questions in a new combination seems to kill two birds with one stone.

If I were hired to teach in a new district, I'd want to know not only whether the test was norm-referenced or criterion-referenced, and whether it was standards-based, I'd also have other questions. I'd want to know how the test scores were being reported to the public. My expectation would be that the percentile scores rather than the raw scores would be publicized. But, *which* percentile scores would be publicized? That is, would the public know a school's or district's *average* scores, or would it only know the number of children who passed the test? I'd want to know whether reports showed rises in scores within the bottom quartile, or within the top quartile. Obviously, all of this would have ramifications. If, for example, I learned that in my new district, rises in the bottom (or top) quartile scores go totally unreported to the public, I'd worry that support services might be unfairly directed toward children who scored in the second quartile and who were therefore considered to be close to that all-important 50th percentile passing line.

I'd also want to know exactly which scores, and from which parts of the test, were included in the percentile rankings. Do all components of the test count in the percentile ranking? If not, which components *do* count? In one Midwestern state, for example, reading tests involve very long passages, each followed by about thirty questions. Some of these questions aim to reveal a child's general knowledge of language and literature, and these questions are not counted in percentile scores for a school's ranking. On that test, only the comprehension questions are taken into account in determining a child's percentile rank. In another Midwestern state, one third of a particular test involves multiple-choice questions. This component was developed through collaboration with McGraw-Hill, the author of Terra Nova and other norm-referenced tests. The other components of the test involve more extended answers and some writing passages. The question that needs to be asked about this test is "Will the scores from all three components count equally?" Apparently, the multiple-choice section only will be used to determine the child's national percentile ranking. Will there be any stakes attached to the other sections of the test?

Most of all, I'd want to know whether the scores from all children counted toward a school's rank or whether some students were not in the test pool. In many states, children in bilingual and special-education classes are not included in the school's total scores and do not weigh into the school's rankings. There is a logic behind this. In New York City, for example, certain schools house centralized special-education classes (and others, centralized gifted classes) and children are bused to these classes from across all of the districts. Imagine the unhappiness if the influx of the district's special-education population into a school meant that the entire school received lower scores! (No one complains, of course, when the high-scoring gifted children are bused into a school, thus elevating that school's rankings.)

However, people are realizing that when the scores of certain children don't matter in a school's overall scores, it is entirely possible that these children will end up being given less skilled teachers, less well-equipped classrooms, and fewer opportunities to learn. If the purpose of these tests is to hold teachers and school systems accountable for providing a rigorous and equitable education, it is questionable whether it makes sense to avert our eyes from what schools are doing with certain children. When the test scores of students in special-education and bilingual classes are not included in a school's overall score, some schools inappropriately relegate a great many of their lowish-scoring children to these special classes as a way to erase all traces of these children.

For me, the interesting thing about my course of study on tests was that everything I learned had instant applications to my life. And often times, the more I learned, the more tentative I felt. I had always felt certain that it wasn't fair to test newly-arrived immigrants, but suddenly my opinions were less clear cut. I had always assumed that one standardized test was as bad as another, but now I had new questions, new reservations, about tests. The more I learned, the less confident and clear I felt.

3

When a Concern for Scores Drives the Curriculum

I remember the day my SAT scores arrived in the mail: the anxiety as I tore open the envelope, the gasp as I took in the scores, the frantic mental arithmetic as I calculated how these scores compared with my PSAT scores, my siblings' scores, and the published range of admissible scores at the colleges of my choice.

As teachers, we relive these moments when the envelope arrives carrying our students' test scores. We open it with the same anxiety, we hold our breath, and scan the page with the same gulp-down-the-news tension, our hearts beating with the same hopefulness.

Sometimes the news is bad. This will happen to each one of us, and nothing in life quite prepares us for this. Our heart sinks. For a moment, we feel ourselves losing our grip. Then the human will to survive kicks in, and we reach for a rationale, an explanation: "I had six special-needs kids," we say, listening to hear if our words are convincing. "It was a new test" or "This year's snowstorms made the year crazy," or "My class is too big—what do they expect?"

Sometimes the news seems okay at first, and only later we learn that our scores weren't okay after all. The teachers at P.S. 413 celebrated a fifteen-point rise in their test scores only to learn the next day that the district was sending in an emergency SWAT team. "Why?" the teachers asked, befuddled.

"Because your scores went down," the district office responded. "You went from fifth to seventh place in the district rankings." Meanwhile, the teachers in a wealthy, high-scoring suburb were confident about their students' test scores until they learned that the newspaper planned to alter its ranking system to factor out differences attributable to parental income. In both instances, the illusion of security crumbled and teachers were left reaching for reasons.

There are problems with the way we, as teachers, tend to ratio-nalize declining test scores. The biggest problem is that we rarely believe our own rationalizations. We sputter something about crowded classes, new test formats, student transience, and the like, but deep inside we are convinced that these are feeble excuses, a weak cover-up job. We accept the test scores as accurate measures of our children's reading and of our teaching. We allow ourselves to be indicted by the scores. "Guilty as charged," we think.

I hope the early chapters of this book have already helped read-ers to be more knowledgeable about the limitations and biases of tests, and I hope that every page of the book continues to do this. I hope the book helps us to look at our children's scores and inter-pret them with confidence and supporting data, saying perhaps "The fact that my scores went down has a lot to do with the tran-sience of our student population," or "The test was so different it can almost be regarded as a new test. It was predictable that we went down."

Checking Our Practice

While it is important to be more savvy about the limitations and biases of standardized reading tests, most readers probably believe (as I do) that there is *some* correlation between test scores and read-ing abilities. I certainly don't think a mere ten-point difference in scores between one year's class and the next is attributable to the newest revisions in a teacher's methods of teaching reading. How-ever, if most of a teacher's children were to score in the bottom quartile on standardized reading tests, I would certainly regard this as a reading problem. Biased, inadequate, and faulty as the tests are, it is still true that when children score very poorly on standard-ized tests, this is probably not just a test-taking problem. Although no single score for any one child should be used alone to determine a child's reading progress, if our classroom as a whole isn't scoring anywhere near to our expectations, it is reasonable to examine, not only our methods of test prep but also our methods of teaching reading. It is reasonable to look squarely at our approaches to teaching reading and ask, "What could I have done better?" and "What gaps might there be in my teaching?"

It is almost inevitable that even if *we* don't take a good look at our methods of instruction, others will. I think it is crucial for us as teachers to be ready to respond to low test scores, first by analyzing those scores and then by reflecting critically on our methods of teaching reading, because if we're not willing to rethink our teaching methods, it may be that others end up doing this for us, diagnosing what *they* think is wrong with our teaching and prescribing *their* solutions. We need to initiate and actively participate in discussions of what else we could be doing with our teaching, so that our voices will be the lead voices in these conversations.

It is almost certain that if we teach reading using real books instead of worksheets, and our children respond to books by talking and writing rather than by bubbling and filling in blanks, the public will point to our progressive methods as the cause of low test scores. (When our test scores are high, on the other hand, our children's success will be attributed to other factors entirely.) It will be the case that when our students' scores drop—and it is inevitable that someday scores will go down—people will descend on us from all sides, pushing their instant solutions for improving test scores. With tremendous assurance, people will point out why our methods have led to the demise of standards, and they will present their prescriptions: "Buy this program." "Follow this teacher's manual." "Use these materials."

It is wise for us progressive teachers especially to be ready for the day when we are called upon to "explain" our children's reading scores. I am by no means suggesting that progressive teachers encounter more problems in their methods of teaching reading than do teachers who follow basal and drill-and-skill programs. But I do think that progressive teachers have a special responsibility for looking critically at our own methods. Because we challenge the status quo of teaching reading, because we determine our own reading curricula and methods of teaching, we are particularly vulnerable. We need to be sure our teaching stands on solid ground.

Just as teachers reach for explanations for a dip in test scores, so does the public. If children in a classroom, a school, or a community do worse than people expect, the public wants to know why. The public wants to hear that there is a program, a teaching method, or an administrator to blame or discard.

It is predictable that low scores on standardized reading tests will lead people to question an existing reading curriculum. The rhetoric behind tests is that they exist to hold teachers, principals, and school districts accountable. It would be good if the rhetoric behind tests were also about holding communities responsible for giving all children equal access to books, to literate mentors, to small classes, to opportunities to tell and hear stories. Instead, the public believes that standardized tests are necessary because they hold educators to higher standards. When reading scores are low, people assume the culprit is the reading curriculum. I suspect the public finds solace in the illusion that there is a single culprit. Once the culprit has been identified and nailed, the public can think, "Now life and reading scores will improve."

Feeling Pressure from Criticism

These days the public need not spend a great deal of time looking for and thinking through explanations for the low scores. The media have already made the diagnosis. A recent article in *Time* magazine (Collins, 1997) suggests that children nationally attain low scores because they are receiving inadequate phonics instruction, and that the fault for this lies with progressive, whole language methods of teaching reading. An article in *The Atlantic Monthly* (Lemann, 1997) echoed these sentiments, as have hundreds of articles like it across the country.

There is an air of tremendous confidence in the media coverage of the "crisis" in teaching reading. References are made to "reliable, replicable research," and the claims of researchers who favor direct skills instruction are supported with supposedly irrefutable evidence. Thus, it is tempting to believe that higher reading scores for our students can be achieved by replacing progressive teaching methods with drill-and-skill methods. Although many of us are reluctant to subject our children to a steady diet of worksheets, drills, exercises, and the like, public pressure for high test scores is so intense that some teachers wonder whether they have any choice but to resort to these methods of teaching.

In good times, when we are at our strongest, we can maintain our critical facilities, looking over the proposed solutions with a discerning eye, judging them against our beliefs about how children learn to read. That is hard to do when our children's test scores have gone down, when deep inside we are already thinking, "How did I mess up?" Teachers I know sometimes end up thinking, "Should I forsake all that I believe in so as to teach for better scores? Are improved test scores that important to me?" "What, ultimately, matters most to me as a teacher? Do I care so much about higher test scores that I'll give up trying to produce thoughtful, avid readers?"

It is unfortunate that these teachers accept as a given the critics' assertion that drill-and-skill methods of teaching reading produce better scores on standardized reading tests than literature-based methods. In the face of pressure from the public and administrators, they come to believe that the best way to achieve higher test scores is to follow drill-and-skill curricula, preferably those written by test publishers and those that require kids to practice the same kinds of tasks in the same kinds of conditions as those on the test. The assumption that the most efficient method to raise test scores is to follow a curriculum that mimics the tests is so widespread that we need to ask if there is any logic behind it.

Is There a Reading Crisis?

We must first address the notion that children in the United States today are failing as readers in new and dramatic ways, and question, if this so, whether the fault lies with progressive, literacy-based, whole language, child-centered methods of teaching reading.

This is not true. Wrong. I can say this with total assurance because it is a fallacy that more US children are failing as readers now than ever before. In fact, there is no conclusive evidence that children are reading worse today than at any other time in this nation's history.

Unbelievable! Everywhere we turn, people are discussing the causes of the crisis in the teaching of reading. How could all these people be wrong? Is there *truly* no reading crisis? How can a logical, clear-headed person believe this?

These were my thoughts exactly. But I have come to believe three things. First, the media matter. The myth that children are failing as readers in new and dramatic ways has been published by many reputable sources. There was a basis for these claims—such as a decline in verbal SAT scores between 1955 and 1996. Although researchers have since shown that the decline in SAT scores doesn't demonstrate a reading crisis, the claims that children are failing in new ways were already out there in print, and they take on a life of their own. One journalist cites another. Soon it becomes common knowledge that our children are failing as readers. Once conclusions are printed, they become accepted. They are circulated, quoted, cited, and thought of as common knowledge.

At the same time, we have to acknowledge that a reading crisis, although it is not new and is not in the forms or for the reasons the media claim, does exist. Particularly when I work in city classrooms, I am often knocked flat by the recognition that many, many children are progressing through our schools without becoming confident, strong readers. Yes, there is a reading crisis. This is especially horrifying in today's world because the demands on people as readers are escalating. As Steven Krashen (1996) has put it, the auto mechanic of today needs to be a far stronger reader than the auto mechanic of yesterday. Then, too, we can see a crisis in the fact that children who can read are growing up choosing never to read. Jim Trelease (1995) cites a study of 25,000 literate fifth graders that shows they spend 33 percent of their free time watching television and 1 percent of their free time reading. Yes, there is a reading crisis. Yes, we are right to be alarmed. But no, this is not a *new* reading crisis.

Finally, I've come to believe it serves some people well to tell the story of education today as if we were in a new state of crisis, because then they can gallop in on white horses as the saviors of American schools. I see these saviors thundering in on the scene nationally, and most of us, as teachers, find these saviors thundering into our classrooms, our curriculum, our parent conferences, espousing whatever their solutions might be.

It is critical, then, that when people claim to know how and why American children are doing so much worse in reading, we show some skepticism. American children are reading as well today as at any time in our country's history. One book that discusses this is *The Manufactured Crisis: Myths, Fraud, and the Attack on America's Public Schools* (Berliner & Biddle, 1995). As Jeff McQuillan (1998), author of *The Literary Crisis: False Claims, Real Solutions* puts it, "What is striking about reading achievement scores in the United States over the past twenty-five years is not how they've declined, but just how *stable* they have been. Several researchers have reviewed and published detailed analyses of the state of reading in the United States, and nearly all of them have come to the same conclusion: children in the United States are reading as well now as they did a generation ago, and maybe better" (p. 6).

The findings from these books and from other research were laid out in a research meeting at a 1997 National Council of Teachers of English Conference. The speaker, Michael Kibby, first tackled the myth of declining SAT scores. He showed a graph suggesting there has indeed been a dramatic dip in the verbal SAT scores. However, he reminded us, taking these tests is voluntary. The commonly reproduced graph that suggests there has been a decline in test scores does not show the fact that when the scores were higher, only 3 percent of high school seniors took the test, many of them students at private schools such as Exeter, Choate, and Andover. Now, more than 40 percent of high school seniors take the tests. Because this is a voluntary test and the population taking the test is not consistent, the SAT scores from long ago cannot be compared with those of today. In his book *Student Literacy*, Kibby says, "The SAT is useless for evaluating changes in academic performance; and any educator, journalist, or politician who uses SAT results as an index of change in educational achievement does so in ignorance or for reasons that must be considered suspect" (1995). He goes on to say that although it's not credible to cite declining average SAT test scores as evidence that our students' reading abilities are declining, people continue to do so. "The media and the last four Secretaries of Education have used SAT scores in this manner, thus perpetuating and increasing the public's misunderstanding of American students' literacy, numeracy, and general knowledge" (Kibby, 1995). The decline in SAT reading scores cannot be used as evidence that there is a reading crisis among our students today.

Kibby also points to several forms of data that *do* reliably show long-term trends. One way researchers have to find trends over time is to give the children of today the tests of yesterday and compare the scores. For example, in 1976, Roger Farr and Leo Ray at Indiana University tested 16,000 tenth graders with the Iowa Silent Reading Test from 1945. In 1986 they administered this same test to 8,000 sixth graders and 8,000 tenth graders. The children of today scored higher than the children of yesterday by a statistically significant amount.

There have been thirty-three then-and-now assessments of children's learning, and all but one concluded that children then did not score as well on comparable reading tests as children now (Kibby, 1995).

Another source of data is a test known as the NAEP, or National Assessment of Educational Progress. The NAEP Long-Term Trends test has received a lot of national attention lately because it was scores from this test, ranked by state, that highlighted California's alleged reading problems. California's children scored the lowest in the nation on the test, which led some Californians (and some media) to name progressive educational methods as the culprit. What the public rarely hears is that the NAEP Long-Term Trends test has been administered nine times since 1971, and when comparing nine-year-olds in 1971 to those in 1996, national scores show that the performance of nine-year-old children today is statistically better than the performance of the same age group in 1971 (Katzman and Hodas, 1995). This is also true for thirteen-year-olds. Scores achieved by older students—aged seventeen—show no statistically significant changes over the past fifteen years, but here again, today's scores are at least as strong as yesterday's scores.

In his new book, McQuillan elaborates on this. He includes tables and describes them, saying,

> Table 1.1 shows the reading scores of U.S. children at three age levels from the first year the NAEP was administered, 1971, to the most recent administration in 1996. The test is scored on a scale of 0 to 500. It is immediately apparent that, despite a few minor fluctuations, reading achievement has either stayed even or increased slightly over the past three decades. There has been no decline whatsoever at any level. (1998, p. 7)

Table 1-1   Average Reading Proficiency of Nine-, Thirteen-, and Seventeen-Year-Olds in the United States, 1971–1996. Source: Campbell, Reese, O'Sullivan, & Dossey (1996), p. 106; Campbell, Voelkl, & Donahue (1997), p. 6.

	1971	1975	1980	1984	1988	1990	1992	1994	1996
Age 9	208	210	215	211	212	209	211	211	212
Age 13	255	256	259	257	258	257	260	258	259
Age 17	285	286	286	289	290	290	290	288	287

Researchers for the prestigious Rand Corporation is another voice in the chorus. They compared students' achievements in 1970 and 1995 (Hanania, 1995), and found that achievement in reading and math is higher today than in 1970 among all groups. African-American and Hispanic children have made the greatest gains.

A number of other sources of data suggest that U.S. children today read as well as they ever have. Readers who want more information about this can consult *The Manufactured Crisis: Myths, Fraud, and the Attack on America's Public Schools* (Berliner & Biddle, 1995). For now, let us turn our attention to the claim that progressive, whole language, child-centered, literature-based approaches to teaching reading are the source of whatever reading crisis *does* exist in schools today.

Research: "Drill-and-Skill" Versus "Literature-Based"

Simply put, there is no conclusive evidence that warrants people making the claim that "new-fangled" methods of teaching reading are responsible for low test scores, or that "drill-and-skill" methods would raise them. On the contrary, there are many studies that support the opposite claim, that children educated in constructivist, literature-based classrooms do better on any reading test than do children in classrooms filled with short-answer questions, worksheets, and decontextualized work on skills.

In fact, a number of recent studies (including Freppon, 1991) have demonstrated clearly that when students have time to read "comprehensible text" (that is, books they can make sense of, books that match their own reading levels), they do as well and usually better on reading tests that assess comprehension. (These students do not necessarily do better on tests that assess their abilities to decode lists of nonsense words.)

Furthermore, studies have shown that when children read a lot, their grammar, spelling, writing, vocabulary, and general knowledge as well as their reading all become stronger. Stephen Krashen (1997) summarizes the research on this topic and says, "Good scores come from the flashlight-under-the-blanket phenomenon." He adds, "This is the Nancy Drew meets the Hardy

Boys on Fear Street method of teaching reading." One study cited by Krashen is Sandra Pitzer's work with underprepared college freshman. Pitzer knew about the studies showing that when K–2 kids are read to, they do overwhelmingly better on any test of reading. She wondered whether this came from hearing the language of stories, from sensing how stories are put together, or something else. She decided to read aloud to her underprepared college freshman. Then she found that the books she read began disappearing from every nearby library. How do we get children and young adults to read? By helping them to love reading, by helping them to get hooked on books. Krashen (1996) also reviewed research showing that students in silent sustained reading programs make very strong gains in reading comprehension if the program lasts long enough. He tells about a 1975 study of sixth-grade boys by Greanney and Clark; the boys participated in a free reading program in their school for a year. Six years later, those children were reading more than comparison students. Connie Weaver and her colleagues have also summarized studies showing that literature-based, whole language approaches to reading lead to strong scores on standardized reading tests (Weaver, Gillmeister-Krause & Vento-Zogby, 1996).

Earlier, I mentioned the NAEP test, which had led to mayhem over scores in California. Fourth-grade teachers across the United States were asked to characterize their reading instruction, and the teachers' responses were compared with students' scores on the NAEP test. Students whose teachers described their approaches as whole language received an average score of 220 on the test, while students in phonics-based classrooms received a lower average score of 208—a statistically significant difference (Mullis, Campbell, & Farstrup, 1993).

Margaret Moustafa reviewed these and other findings in her book, *Beyond Traditional Phonics: Research Discoveries and Reading Instruction* (1997). In this book, she describes method comparison studies of first-grade classrooms and classrooms of high-risk children and non-native speakers. Most of these studies show whole language children doing better than skills-based children not only on comprehension but also on word-attack skills. In Freppon's (1991) study of two first-grade classrooms, for example, children who were taught to regard reading as constructing meaning with print were twice as successful as children in traditional classrooms at sounding out words. In a comparative study examining the effects of instruction on test scores for two groups, one who used a whole language approach to teaching reading, and one who used a phonics-only approach, Manning and Long (1989) found that children in the whole language classroom did better on the Stanford Achievement subtest of word parts, even though children in the skills classroom had explicitly studied word parts.

Krashen (1996) cites forty other studies of sustained silent reading. In thirty-eight of these, sustained silent reading students equaled or outperformed traditionally taught comparison students on tests of reading comprehension. Krashen writes, "Results were even more positive for longer-term studies (longer than seven months) (p. 12). McQuillan concurs that studies have shown that having time for real reading, inside or outside the classroom, tends to improve scores:

> International comparisons show the same strong effects of print access on reading achievement. Elley's (1994, 1996) comparison of reading score, home environment, and school and public library data from several countries came to the conclusion that *access to print was the most powerful correlate of reading achievement.* Controlling for differences in economic conditions among the participating countries, Elley (1996) found that the size of the school library was the number one factor distinguishing the reading scores of nine-year-olds between the high and low scoring nations, with an impressive effect size of .82. Frequent silent reading time was the next most important variable, with an effect size of .78. (McQuillan, 1998, p. 120–127)

Of course, some research studies have been used to support a phonics-only approach to teaching reading. Moustafa explains in *Beyond Traditional Phonics* (1997) that researchers such as Jeanne Chall, Guy Bord and Robert Dykstra, Isabelle Liberman and her colleagues, and many others have found that children who do well on tests that assess knowledge of letters and phonemes tend to be more proficient readers (see Adams, 1990, for further review). Moustafa points out that the problem with interpreting these findings to mean that letter-phoneme knowledge is of the utmost importance in reading is that correlation doesn't establish causation. Just because skilled readers know their phonemes doesn't mean that drill on phonemes is the best way to create a nation of skilled readers.

Many studies, then, suggest that access to books and time to read independently chosen books are crucial factors leading to higher test scores. But this doesn't dismiss all the arguments against literature-based progressive teaching.

We have all heard about progressive teachers who failed to hold kids accountable for doing good work. We have heard of well-intentioned, creative teachers who filled their classrooms with sofas and books, yet neglected to give their children the reading skills necessary to achieve on tests or in life. There are ineffective teachers following both progressive and skill-and-drill approaches. But teachers who take control of teaching into their own hands are in a more vulnerable position than those who follow the script laid out by publishers in textbooks and teacher's guides. The teachers who teach using children's literature are relying on their own knowledge bases, and this makes them responsible and vulnerable. It is rare to hear people criticizing the curricula of teachers who follow conservative, middle-of-the-road, teach-by-the-book approaches. Most teachers do follow a basal textbook curriculum, and yet it's clearly not the case that they are all successful at achieving higher scores for all their students. But it's rare for such teachers and programs to be held culpable.

Raising Test Scores by Making the Curriculum Match the Test

Administrators, parents, teachers, and the media often argue that the most certain way to guarantee that tests scores go up in a modestly effective teacher's class is for that teacher to follow a prescribed curriculum written by the very people who write the standardized test the children will take. It makes sense to think that the way to increase tests scores is to ensure that instruction mimics the test. There is, in fact, some truth to this. Ted Chittenden, Jacqueline Jones, and Beverly Falk have all helped my colleagues and me to realize that this is the reason that whenever a new test is introduced, children tend not to score well at first. Over the following three years, teachers narrow and realign their instruction so that it imitates the test more closely, and scores go up. The rise in scores doesn't necessarily reflect stronger reading abilities—the rise often disappears when a different test is introduced. What the rise does reflect is a closer alignment between the teaching method and the test. But it is universal and predictable that after a several-year rise, scores will plateau again. (At which point, my test advisers tell me, politicians and administrators are apt to switch to a new "more rigorous" test, anticipating the same three-year rise in scores and thereby "proving" how much they have improved the education system in their area.)

The belief that literature-based approaches to teaching reading won't yield high test scores also persists in part because there will always be progressive teachers of literature-based curricula for whom standardized reading test scores are low and have not risen. Usually, this happens because these teachers have been unsupported and uninformed about the solid, rigorous practices of teaching reading in a constructivist classroom.

If a teacher is uninformed and unsupported, she may have more success, both in teaching reading and in raising test scores, by following a highly scripted, step-by-step, minute-by-minute formula than by being given total autonomy and encouraged to rely on her own ideas. To give teachers the authority to teach in ways they see fit is to expect that they are well-prepared professionals—in short, to ask that they know how to teach reading. In districts where people don't believe their teachers can live up to the job of teaching reading, and in districts where people won't pay for, or wait for, teachers to develop these professional skills, the packaged, formulaic programs are an alternative. That is, there is some truth to the argument that a quick-fix way for a principal to raise scores in a school where levels of teaching are particularly weak is to match the curriculum to the test.

In these cases, the sheer momentum of the prepackaged program with its worksheets, checklists, built-in assessments, and prescribed teacher activities may carry the scores up higher than they are in some literature-based classrooms. Furthermore, teachers and administrators sometimes teach and lead with more confidence when a freshly printed, neatly packaged, extensively structured, expensive program stands behind them. That, too, can push scores up higher than they would be with a more individualized system of preparing for the tests. Yet I am *in no way* recommending this practice. What follows is my emerging understanding of why this practice is both unethical and damaging to children in the long run.

As Linda Darling-Hammond (1989) once put it, imagine that to check on the effectiveness of doctors, we took the temperature of every one of their patients all at once to see how many registered "normal." Then imagine that all the doctors ran around just before-hand giving their patients huge doses of aspirin and putting them in chilly rooms, and giving them cold drinks right before the thermometers went in. Would the results of the test tells us much about the health of the patients? About the healing skills of the doctors? Everyone would have to agree that this means of preparing for the test would destroy any validity the test might have. So it is, also, for certain means of preparing children for reading tests. Beverly Falk recently directed me to an article that proposes two evaluative standards to check on the appropriateness of any given test preparation program (Popham, 1991). The first seems obvious: "No test preparation practice should violate the ethical standards of the education profession." Or, simply put, no changing student answers, leaking the test ahead of time, copying, or other blatant transgressions of the rules. The second standard reads, "No test preparation practice should increase students' test scores without simultaneously increasing student mastery of the content domain tested." In other words, don't lower a patient's temperature without improving her health; don't raise a child's test scores without improving his reading abilities.

This is not to say that all preparation for tests is unethical. On the contrary, as Popham says, "Generalized . . . special instruction on how to take tests allows students' test performance to be more accurately reflective of their true state of knowledge and/or skill." This kind of test preparation, as we know, can prevent students from being confused or intimidated by a strange format or the requirements of tests.

Clearly, however, the kind of test preparation/reading curriculum advocated by some districts is unethical by these standards, particularly when the same publisher writes the reading curriculum (the basal) and then writes the test by which not only children but also teaching methods will be judged. This is not exactly fair. Why would tests be whisked away from teachers so as to ensure that the next time students take the test they are all equally disadvantaged, when at the same time a publisher writes a curriculum that will be evaluated based on the tests that he has in his hands? In talking about this with my colleagues, I came to realize that this would be rather like a bunch of teachers getting hold of a copy of the test in August, making hundreds of versions with slight variations, then calling this pile "our reading curriculum." After a year of following this course, the kids would be all set, in artificially boosted conditions, for the test.

Even if we wanted to, we teachers can't get ahold of the tests our kids will take. But the same people who publish the test *do* publish the reading curriculum that sets kids up for the tests. These publishers hail the fact that—lo and behold!—children who have run through their curricula often do at least modestly well on the tests. Is it ethical to prepare children for tests in this way? Is it ethical for the testing companies to be making money by selling a curriculum that matches the tests to which only they have access?

Adding insult to injury, these test-publishing companies also claim that because their "reading curriculum" often leads kids to higher scores on the same company's tests, their curriculum is the most rigorous way to teach reading. In fact, as Lauren Resnick (1994) has written, the very fact that this kind of test preparation can significantly improve reading scores is proof that the tests do not test how well a child can read but in fact test how well she can take a reading test. The fact that aligning the curriculum with the test has some short-term payoff in higher test scores is not doubted, but when companies further use this fact to claim that their curriculum is the most effective way to nurture readers, we have to be outspokenly critical of this claim. To be successful in further education and to live literate lives, children need to develop strengths as readers that will not necessarily show up on standardized reading tests.

So, if it is true that one way to create at least a temporary rise in test scores is to follow a curriculum that mimics the test, it is important to remember that, in fact, data suggest that a more effective and long-lasting way to achieve high scores is to follow a curriculum that fosters in students a deep understanding and fluency in the actual process of reading. Teachers do not have to abandon a literature-based method of teaching that requires kids to read and respond to books in order to achieve higher test scores. As I have mentioned, there are many studies that have shown that students who are given lots of time to read real books and who are expected to talk and write extensively in response to those books are more likely to receive higher scores on standardized reading tests than students from drill-and-skill classrooms. Whatever they are called— literature-based, constructivist, whole language—methods that involve more reading lead to higher test scores on any test that involves reading comprehension (Krashen, 1996).

Narrowly Focused Reading Curricula Can Be Harmful

Teaching to tests may achieve higher scores in the short run, but these scores are *not* evidence that the kids are strong readers. In fact, this kind of program may have deprived the students of valuable time they could have spent in learning to read; it might also have limited their reading knowledge to the point that they will score even more poorly on other kinds of standardized reading tests.

It's a terrible thing to so constrict the reading curriculum that the only things taught are those skills that can fit into a multiple-choice, short-answer reading test. When teachers teach to that kind of test, they have embraced a narrow view of learning. They teach only what is tested, and only in the forms and formats used by the tests. This leads teachers to emphasize superficial content, rote drill, and discrete skills at the expense of in-depth projects and other thought-provoking tasks. Teaching to the tests begets classwork in which students spend their time answering multiple-choice or fill-in-the-blank questions rather than on more challenging types of work, like writing essays, conducting research, experimenting, reading and discussing literature, debating, solving difficult problems, and creating products (Boyer, 1983; Darling-Hammond, 1990, 1991; Darling-Hammond & Wise, 1985; Goodlad, 1984; Kantrowitz & Wingert, 1989; NAEYC, 1988). Efforts to teach to the tests have led to the development of curricula based on transmittal of isolated, decontextualized facts (Boyer, 1983) and have promoted student passivity (Goodlad, 1984) and rote memorization (McKnight et al., 1987). When classwork is oriented toward recognizing the answers to multiple-choice questions, students' proficiency in aspects of learning that are not tested, such as analysis, complex problem solving, and written and oral expression, has been severely limited (Darling-Hammond & Wise, 1985; Haney & Madaus, 1986; Koretz, 1988; NAEP, 1981).

A narrow focus on testing skills deprives children of the substance of literacy. Good reading requires knowledge about the world, context, meaning, and phonics. Many of the strategies that support good test taking are counterproductive to those we use when we read competently. Good readers, for example, take lots of risks in the process of reading most materials. These risks lead to errors. Depending upon their impact on meaning, these errors may or may not be corrected by the reader. But reading tests, which involve fairly short passages followed by trick questions and answers, require being constantly alert to precisely the kind of insignificant errors that good readers let fall to the wayside (Edelsky, 1991; Meier, 1991;).

Across the country, teachers have seen for themselves that narrow test preparation in the place of real reading education is harmful to students. In a district in New Jersey, teachers and administrators in one junior high school decided to put all their energy into a test preparation curriculum for their students. They followed a program designed specifically for the test their students would take. Within two years, their students had the highest scores in the area on that reading test. The sad ending to the story is that when these same kids went to high school, one third of them had to be placed in remedial reading classes. It was as if the children had been given steroids to artificially boost their short-term performance.

Another school in New York City also had a problem with low reading scores. The teachers and principal decided that from the first day of the school year they would each conduct at least one hour per day of preparation for the cloze-type test, in which selected words are missing and must be filled in by the student from a list of choices. As in the case of the other school, this intense preparation did help the kids on the cloze test. Unfortunately, since the kids had not learned to be better readers, nor had they learned general test-taking skills, when the citywide test changed, the scores of that school were lower than ever before.

When test preparation dominates the entire reading curriculum, the resulting damage can be extensive. Will a child who has learned about reading through hundreds of fill-in-the-blank exercises be the kind of child who reads books by flashlight under the covers at night?

4

The Overlap of Good Teaching and Good Test Scores

All educators will agree, at least publicly, that we don't want to raise children's reading scores without teaching them to read. What is not generally agreed upon is how to teach children reading in a way that will increase their scores.

For the past twenty years people have been hearing that there is *this* way to teach reading, or *that* way—that there are two roads, a right one and a wrong one, with only an unprincipled, wishy-washy muddle in between. Closer to the truth is that a good many people have found value in some of the undeniable tenets of both paths of thinking about literacy education: that children need to spend time reading, that they need to be read to, and that most children benefit from clear instruction in the ways of turning marks on the page into meaningful language. There are many ways to enact these tenets in order for children to learn to read.

When schools work as communities of learners—and many of them do this well—they become places where teachers as well as children learn. Teachers who sit together around the big table in their staff rooms talk a lot with each other about children and what they need, and in these conversations they hear about a whole range of practical, classroom-based strategies. As a result, many teachers across the country have seen validity in progressive methods as well as in the practices of solid traditional teaching. They have created their beliefs and practices from both.

This practice of drawing from both extremes of theory about the teaching of reading contrasts with the image of a divided field of teaching projected by the media. It may be that some publishers or politicians have a stake in escalating a "reading war" but most teachers, meanwhile, mostly want a wider repertoire of ways to help their children learn.

Most reading teachers will agree that to teach children to read, we need to be sure certain conditions exist: children should have access to reading material, have materials read to them, have opportunities to talk about and make sense of what they read or hear, receive instruction in the ways of turning print into meaning, and be frequently assessed in order to match the teaching and the texts to their needs.

My colleagues and I spend most of our professional lives observing and coaching teachers who are trying to teach reading well, usually with a constructivist, child-centered, literature-based approach that includes solid, direct instruction about making sense of print and other things. We have come to believe there are a handful of recommendations we can make to these teachers for both strengthening their reading curricula and improving their test scores. Teachers who want to improve their students' scores on standardized reading tests will want to begin by conducting a thoughtful review of their reading curricula in the light of the issues we raise here.

Putting More Reading in the Reading Curriculum: Using Art, Writing, and Talk to Focus on, Not Distract from, Reading

The children in Ms. Hines' first-grade classroom were engrossed in a thematic unit on food. As part of that study, the children pored over the small print on food cans and packages in the kitchen cupboards at home. "This is unbelievable!" one boy announced to his mother. Looking up from scrutinizing a package of dried chicken soup mix, he exclaimed, "There's no chicken in the chicken soup!" A few minutes later, he was even more mystified. "Can you believe it?" he marveled. "There's no chocolate in the chocolate jimmies either!"

Around the Teachers College Reading and Writing Project community, this child's discovery soon became a metaphor to describe a common pitfall in many reading curricula. Just as there is sometimes no chicken in the chicken soup and no chocolate in the chocolate jimmies, sometimes there is no reading in the reading curriculum.

Startling as this may sound, the truth is that many children read for a remarkably small percentage of the school day. Researchers have for a long while documented that children in many classrooms spend more time on dittos and exercises, multiple-choice questions, and language drills than on reading whole texts. Children sometimes spend two-and-a-half hours a day in reading instruction and only ten minutes of that time actually reading. Many of us know of classrooms in which *sustained* silent reading lasts for only ten minutes a day! This, in and of itself, hints at the problem. But there are other reasons why children often don't read in school. Besides spending their time on dittos and word games, in some classrooms children spend a good portion of their reading instruction time doing literature-based arts and crafts. The arts and crafts vary depending on the age of the child, but may include

- making dioramas, game boards, posters, or mobiles to accompany a book
- making toilet-paper-roll puppets to reenact the story
- making new books with new illustrations that are innovations or variations on the original books
- filling bulletin boards with murals or other artwork about an author or a story

Art

Teachers are apt to describe this artwork as "responses to literature," and sometimes it is just that. Sometimes probing inquiries arise around the artwork, with children rereading portions of the text, debating the images they have developed from the text, citing the rationale behind their decisions, and so forth. More often, though, the conversations during the painting and cutting and papier-mâché revolve around the smells of different flavors of magic markers, the little wax fingercaps children make with glue, or the "yucky" lumps they feel in the papier-mâché.

One rationale for having children invest time in artwork during reading workshop is that they are interpreting the story using multiple ways of knowing. Then, too, in classrooms filled with emergent or reluctant readers, artwork provides a reading-related activity that can keep three quarters of the class busy and relatively quiet while the classroom teacher reads with a small group of children. Third, the artwork functions as a reward for the hard work of reading, talking, or writing in response to a book. When all that hard work is completed, children can do a culminating project. The project becomes the "spoonful of sugar to help the medicine go down." Finally, art projects are tangible and active. If students make a mural or a book jacket or a question-and-answer game, this makes reading into something less abstract. We can see and hold and hang up and evaluate reading more easily when there is an accompanying product.

I sympathize with these motivations for spending reading time doing artwork, but I question this use of time. My colleagues and I were skeptical about the idea of spending reading workshop time on art projects even before we began to consider how our reading classrooms might better help children score well on standardized tests, but the presence of the tests makes us all the more convinced.

I think it's arguable that *nothing* in the school day matters more to a child's education than time for children to read, with the teacher there to instruct and coach. If children become readers, if they develop the habit of gulping down lots and lots of texts, they'll probably end up having a wider knowledge of history, science, vocabulary, grammar, geography, current events, and so on. Reading truly is a magic carpet that can take our students anywhere.

Yet children in the United States rarely read. In his *Read-Aloud Handbook* (1995), Jim Trelease cites a study showing that literate fifth graders spend 33 percent of their free time watching television and 1 percent of their free time reading books (and this includes the time they spend on homework!). Researchers have clearly established that the best way to ensure children read at home is to be sure they read in school. If children get engrossed in books at school, and then bring those same books home with them, they are more apt to read at home. What could matter more?

I know that some teachers—especially in the primary grades—will respond, "Yes, but my children *can't* carry on independently as readers yet. They can only read when I am with them." Frequently, therefore, these teachers set up reading workshops in which children spend time in centers doing art projects, dittos, and the like. The teachers, meanwhile, may meet with a small group of readers to walk through a text together.

The curious thing is that we no longer say this about writing. We don't say, "My children can't, you know, *write*." Instead we've come to believe that all children can write independently *as best they can write*. Some may be approximating writing, but still we invite them to act as writers within our classrooms and in their lives. Our teaching consists of drawing our chairs alongside children as they write, watching what they do, and intervening to lift the level of their work. We don't say to our youngsters as writers, "Why don't you make a puppet and when I have time, I'll gather five of you together and then we can *write* a story, beginning to end, together."

I am convinced that just as even very young children can carry on as writers, working collaboratively and independently, so, too, all our children can carry on as readers. It may be that some of our most emergent readers will spend time in the reading workshop poring over pictures, pretend-reading (approximating reading), or singing the songs of books they know well, but all of this has more to do with reading than making a diorama in a shoebox.

I also reject the argument that if an art project is motivating, it helps children love reading. If it's true that the chance to make a papier-mâché map of Sarah's journeys in *Sarah, Plain and Tall* is more fun for children than reading the book (and I question that this is the case), doesn't this art project do just the opposite of what we intend? If our children sit through the reading part of a reading workshop yearning for the chance to cut, paste, and paint, how does this turn children into people who love to curl up with a book? I don't want the chance to glue and scissor to be "the spoonful of sugar"; I want the story itself to be the reward, and I am convinced it can be.

It is harder for me to address the fact that sometimes we have our children work on art projects during reading workshop because we want to turn reading into something tangible and concrete. I think many teachers feel insecure when their children are *just* reading. Somehow, if each of our students is hunkered over a book, we feel as if we're not doing our job. "How can we be sure they are really reading?" And if they are reading, and we don't know the book, we wonder, "What's there to teach?"

I do believe that teachers deserve help in knowing how to actively, assertively intervene to lift the level of a child's reading. We need help in knowing what the quality in reading consists of once a child can read. I'll address this later in this chapter; for now, I hope it's enough to say that although the artwork may turn a book into something concrete, it's questionable whether the artwork has turned *reading* into something concrete. Perhaps, instead, the artwork has lured children away from the very thing we are trying to support. There are ways to help us focus the artwork children do during reading time to angle it more toward deepening their reading and less toward distracting them from it. In all cases, it seems likely that the art has deepened the reading if, after working on the art, the reader's image of the reading changes, or if further reading leads the child to change the artwork. The following are some focusing strategies:

- Children try to draw a picture of something in a story and refer back constantly to a description in the text to keep their vision on track. Students might try to imagine Lyra's world in Philip Pullman's *The Golden Compass,* reworking their drawings as they move through the text and get a clearer and clearer picture of it.
- Children come to a better understanding of the world of a story by mapping it out. Students who are struggling with holding the world of the story in their minds as they read from day to day might sketch the important scenes from each day's reading and refer back to those scenes to reenter the text the next day.
- Children sketch a family tree to help them understand the family relationships in a tale. For example, students might have trouble keeping track of all the characters in Walter Dean Myers' *The Glory Field* and might need to create a chart or sketch to keep them sorted out.
- Children draw a graphic organizer to help them keep straight the information they are gathering from reading. Students might create charts to compare the characters in their books or to compare one text to another. They might chart the happy and sad parts of the books to try to think about how characters change over the course of a story.

Writing

Often, of course, children are *not* spending a lot of their reading class time on artwork. But even so, it's not necessarily the case that there is a great deal of reading going on. Sometimes when I visit a classroom during reading time, I walk into the room and do a double take. "Is this reading?" I sometimes ask the teacher. "Or is it writing? I'd wanted to come during reading, not writing." The teacher may nod proudly and tell me that, yes, indeed, this is a reading class. Then she may go on to tell me that her children are

- writing in their notebooks about the reading they've just done
- writing letters to the author
- writing new variations on the story
- writing their own endings to the story
- writing a diary as if they were a character
- recording the facts of the text

Obviously, there are reasons to spend a bit of time during the reading workshop jotting notes in preparation for a book talk, recording passages one wants to remember for life, and so forth. But I think we, as teachers, need to remember that chances are neither we nor any of the skilled readers we know regularly write summaries of the books we read, letters from one character to another, or new endings for the stories we read. And we need, I believe, to have an unsettled feeling if we look out over a classroom during reading time and see that no one is reading. Writing matters. I am all for children spending time each day writing. I dearly want children to have lots of time to make their own literature. I am convinced that the opportunity to be authors and to create their own pieces will enable children to read more critically and more consciously. But I suspect that writing literature will do more for children's reading than writing *about* literature.

Talk

Why not, instead, have children do what readers the world over do, which is to *talk* in response to texts? Why not have children read in partnerships, where they gather together with a buddy each day to talk about the chapters they've just read? They might meet to talk about Frog and Toad's friendship and how it compares to their own friendship. They might stick Post-it notes on sections of a text to help them get ready for a talk about what it would be like to live in a world like Jonah's in *The Giver*.

Now, there are also predictable problems that occur when children talk about books. One day, while Mr. Murphy's fourth graders were meeting for half of reading time to talk about their books, Kyle told David, "I put a Post-it on my favorite part of the chapter I read." Kyle showed David a sentence about two boys who found flashlights in the basement of their grandfather's house. Kyle and David then spent the next fifteen minutes talking about the amazing games *they* had played with flashlights. The book had completely left their minds and their conversation. At one point, the book literally slipped onto the floor. Neither boy noticed.

In other corners of the classroom, Sarah and Michelle talked about why younger brothers are so difficult, and James and Tyrone discussed what they would wish for if they were to find a lucky pebble. Listening to all this, I couldn't help but note, "There is no 'book' in these book talks." The children were relating to the reading, contextualizing some events for themselves, and developing a sense of excitement about books, but still I wondered whether this was the best way for them to become better readers.

In many classrooms, books are the springboard rather than the center of conversations. The book reminds kids of their own lives, and the conversations are off and running.

I certainly do not mean to suggest that talking about books often becomes a waste of time. In fact, I believe that it's by talking about books that children learn to think about books. By retelling a story, children can take the time to build the world of the story in their minds. By sharing ideas and by being asked to defend those ideas, children can learn to find evidence from the text to support their theses.

Because I do not want anyone to lose trust in book talks, I think it is important that we find ways such as these to put the "book" back into the book talks:

- We can suggest that readers often begin their conversations by retelling what they read and then choosing one part to talk more about. It is probably important that students have their books open while they retell what they have read, turning the pages while they talk. In this way, readers can check to be sure that they are following the thread of the text.
- We can encourage children to reread aloud to each other the sections of the texts they're discussing. It's usually best if students read whole sections of texts to each other, rather than just single sentences. In this way, book talks are more contextualized and more apt to hew closely to the story.
- If readers often zoom in on part of a book, summarize it, and then jump off from it to their lives or their opinions, it may help to ask them to retell not only the point under discussion but also the overall story, so that listeners sense how the part fits into the whole. In this way, children who are participants in the book talk stand a chance of being brought into the book and not just into each other's lives.
- We can coach youngsters to often ask each other for evidence from the text to back up what they are saying. Often in conversations children are heard offering provocative interpretations that are taken as facts by their classmates. For example, we might hear a student declare, "The father in this story is mean," or "The girl, she was wrong to do what she did," without offering any information from the text to support this belief. We probably need to teach our students to ask each other to "prove it" or "show me in the book where you got that idea."
- It helps to teach children that before settling on a topic for discussion they need to ask themselves if this is a topic that could bring them back to the book or lead them to think more deeply about it. Children sometimes find that after a few minutes of talk about a particular topic, they have nothing more to say. This occurs most often when the topic they have chosen is only tangentially related to the text. For example, it is hard for a group of students to have a strong conversation about the father in Lucille Clifton's *The Three Wishes*. They might, in fact, be able to make some guesses, but after that there's nothing to talk about.

There's no evidence from the text about a father and therefore nothing more to talk about.

- We can encourage children to nudge others to talk more and think more about their theories. Students might ask each other to say more about their ideas or to give examples. Students might also try to think about the whole of the book they are reading and think of a really big question to consider.

- It helps if groups have facilitators equipped with phrases to help get the group back on task. It is often helpful if there is one student whose job it is to pay attention to the quality of the conversation and whose role it is to say things like, "What are you thinking, Maritza?" or "We seem to be off the topic" or "You look like you want to say something, David" or "Can you say more about that, Cindy?"

- It helps when children self-evaluate their talks. It is often beneficial for students to reflect on the conversations they've had, trying to name the things they did that went well and should be repeated and the things that need to change. Teachers might help students do this by videotaping, audiotaping, or even just transcribing conversations for the class to listen to and comment on. Students can revisit old book talks asking, "What ideas were abandoned mid-way? How could we have continued that discussion? Which part of the book talk worked the best? What made the difference?" We might also get in the habit of holding very short debriefing sessions with the students just to talk a bit about what went well in conversations.

Creating Challenges in Reading: Choosing the Right Level of Difficulty, Building Stamina, and Studying a Variety of Genres

Choose the Right Level of Difficulty

My colleagues and I have recently worked in a lot of classrooms in which the teachers *do* set aside at least a half hour per day for a reading workshop. In these reading workshops, children are encouraged to choose books and to read, read, read. Several problems sometimes occur in these workshops.

Children very often select books that are much too difficult for them. If a child sits holding onto a Gary Paulsen book, her eyes skimming over the words of the book, and if the child comes away from the book with no plot line, no movies-in-the-mind's-eye, then this reading is destructive to the child. The child can come to expect that books don't make sense. It is a major problem if alarm bells don't even go off in the child's mind when print doesn't generate sense. One reason why this happens is that often we stock our classroom libraries with books chosen for a mythical fifth grader, one who could, but does not, exist in our room. Publishers sometimes package boxes of "fifth-grade books," but these may not be the books that *our* fifth graders need to be reading. One wonderful, dedicated teacher I know was in tears this year when he finally realized that 90 percent of his classroom library was beyond the reading level of all but four of his students. For this teacher and for others, part of the problem was that *he* loves authors such as Gary Paulsen, Mildred Taylor, Katherine Paterson, Patricia MacLachlan, Laurence Yep, Brian Jacques, and Lois Lowry. He's dying for his kids to love these authors, too. Of course, there are brilliant, wonderful authors of books that are more accessible, but this teacher needed to become familiar with the work of, say, Clyde Bulla, Ursula LeGuin (The Catwings series), Sharon Mathis, Beverly Cleary, Dick King Smith, and Patricia Reilly-Giff.

This teacher is not alone. Many of us need to know more about children's books and authors. We need to realize that a 200-page book by Beverly Cleary and an equally long book by Lloyd Alexander are *not* necessarily equal in difficulty. We need to know that even though the *Little House* books are about as fat as Cynthia Voigt's trilogy, those Laura Ingalls Wilder books will be an easier read for most of our children.

Then, too, we need an efficient method for evaluating whether a book is too difficult for a child. When we don't know the books our children are reading, we sometimes feel at a loss. I don't think this is necessary. To me, there are two indicators I look for. The first is a student's level of engagement in a book. If the student is always looking up from a book, if his head is like a revolving fan during reading workshop, then I worry. If, on the other hand, when I say, "Let's gather on the carpet," the student walks to the carpet with her eyes still glued to the text, if she doesn't look up until she's reached the end of that section of text, then I don't worry. If I see a student choosing to continue reading during free time, then I tend not to worry whether the book makes sense to that student. He may miss 20 percent of the story, he may skip over the fact that the dog dies on the second-to-last page of *Stone Fox,* but this doesn't particularly concern me. I'm not worried that the reader may miss one point or get a detail wrong. What concerns me very much is when children are not getting lots and lots of meaning from the texts they read.

The second thing I look for in order to determine whether the book is at the right level for the student is if she can talk about the book she is reading. I want to be able to say, "I don't know this book. What's happening in it?" and to have a child be able to fill me in on the gist of a story. I want to be able to read with the child, whatever the portion of text she is reading, and for her to be able to answer me when I interrupt to ask, puzzled, "Who's Harry? Why's he kicking that rock?"

While some children choose books that are too hard, in many literature-based reading classrooms there are also children who tend to be what our colleague Kathleen Tolan calls cruise-readers. These children generally select fairly easy books to read, and watching them read, one feels as if they are on cruise-control: they zoom effortlessly along through texts that pose few problems for them. I think it might be wise for teachers sometimes to encourage these children to read more difficult books, or for teachers to raise the stakes in book talks so that these cruise-readers learn to think in more probing ways. I think it's wise to help these children learn to deal with harder reading.

Build Stamina

When it comes to tests, there are two reasons it's important to help children deal with difficult reading. First of all, for many children it is challenging to just get through some of the excerpts on the reading tests. This may be because the excerpts are just that— excerpts. It may be because they are poorly written. And it may be because the test is written so that some passages are meant to be above the reading level of most of the test takers. Whatever the reason, it's important for children's success with reading tests and for their lives as readers that all children have some experience reading difficult texts, that is, texts that are a stretch but that, with work, can make sense.

When children read difficult texts, we need to watch and coach them on developing a repertoire of strategies for dealing with difficulty. Too many readers become overwhelmed or passive when faced with difficult texts. We need to help children have strategies for dealing with such texts, including

- asking someone to read sections aloud to you
- reading short chunks of text and then pausing and forcing yourself to say something about what you've read
- rereading with exaggerated expression, perhaps giving the characters in the story voices in your mind
- rereading aloud
- rereading with your finger under the text to keep your eyes and your mind focused

Another reason why it is helpful for us to sometimes nudge children to read difficult texts, or to make more out of the texts they do read, is that in order to answer someone else's questions about a passage, readers need to be good at the very strategies that they are apt to use when trying to learn from a text. That is, if I want to be sure I cull the important lessons from a professional book I'm reading on spelling, I have ways to rev up my brain, to push it into high gear. I have ways to stuff vital information into my head, too, and to try to hold onto it. All of this serves me in good stead when I encounter a reading test. For the test, too, I put my brain into high gear and stuff vital information from the page into my head. This time my motivation is different. I'm not driven by what I want to learn but by what I think the test maker will want me to know. But in both cases it helps me to have had experience doing such things as

- reading a paragraph and saying to myself, "So, this is mainly saying . . ."
- noticing the key facts and statistics so that I can remember them or at least locate them again later

- marking sections of the text with Post-it notes and writing key words on the notes to remind me of what those sections are about

Yet another way to help children in their reading and on reading tests is to help them read a lot in one sitting. Stamina matters a great deal on a reading test. It's a problem if the day a student takes a reading test is the first time he has been expected to continue reading for over an hour. I see lots of reading classrooms where the teachers don't seem to notice or complain if children spend five weeks making their way through a book, perhaps reading a 340-page book at a rate of eight pages a day. I wonder if a child can really keep the world of a book alive in his mind for five weeks. My general inclination is to say that we need to help children progress through books at the rate of one per week or per two weeks. This may mean that some children would be wise to read shorter books for the time being.

I also think that, as teachers, we need at intervals in the year to have a way to keep our eyes on each child's progress through a book. We may, for example, want children to leave a Post-it note in the book at the end of each in-school reading session and each at-home reading session. This will make a child's progress through a book more tangible and more public, and make it more likely that we work with children to build their stamina as readers. We may want our children, when they select and begin a book, to develop a reading plan, to say, "I'll read two chapters every night, and at least one more chapter each day in school. This way I should be done with the book by next Thursday." We can help students build up their reading stamina in the following ways:

- We can, little by little, increase the time our students are expected to read during the in-school reading sessions.
- We can help students find back-up books, that is, texts to turn to when they lose steam in the one they are reading. For example, a child might get tired after reading a chapter of *Shiloh*; to keep reading, the child might turn to a collection of poetry or to the latest copy of *Zillions* magazine.
- Students can be encouraged to devise a plan to read a few more pages each day. They might be taught to put a bookmark or Post-it note on the page they want to read up to in one sitting and then try to push themselves to get there.

- We can discuss with students various ways of keeping oneself going, such as taking quick breaks before you are totally tired, going to the bathroom for a few minutes, stretching and then sitting back down, and so on.
- Children can be asked to reflect on times when they have been able to concentrate for a long interval (perhaps playing video games or watching a movie) and then to recreate in their reading lives the conditions that gave them that stamina.

Study a Variety of Genres

There is another issue that may be worth considering when we think about helping children read better and score better on tests. Often children mostly read fiction, and most of the fiction is either realistic fiction or fantasy. The read-aloud texts in classrooms often fall into same genre. Yet many reading tests are equally or even more apt to be filled with genres such as nonfiction and poetry. If the test scores matter a great deal to us or to our children, it makes sense for us to encourage and even insist that children read a wider variety of genres.

Of course, in order for this to happen, a wide range of genres needs to be available in the classroom for children to read. In order to provide genre varieties, we may need to order books, borrow from other classrooms, solicit from parents, or even call on the local library for help. We may want to say to children, "During our independent reading workshop, would you make a point of reading nonfiction for a while?" Some teachers I know encourage each member of the class to subscribe to a magazine about that child's passions—computers, horses, baseball—and to have the magazine come to the classroom. Some teachers put out calls for booklets of game rules, simple assembly instructions, and recipes, and then give children guidance in reading these forms of print. These formats are often similar to excerpts on reading tests.

When we are trying to raise our students' scores, we may want to think over these observations in light of our own reading curricula:

- Are art, writing, and talk during classroom reading time deepening reading instruction or diverting from it?
- Do the kids have and choose books that are reasonably difficult for them—not too easy and not too hard?

- Are the students learning to maintain their concentration for longer and longer spans of time over more and more pages of reading?
- Have the students become acquainted with different types of texts, such as poetry, memos, scientific books, and instruction manuals?

We'll each undoubtedly want to add our own questions to these. All of us, given the opportunity, will have insights into improving our teaching. All of us have strengths to build on, weaknesses to shore up, changes to make, and higher goals to reach. This seems to be both the burden and the thrill of our profession. There is always a new horizon just over the next hilltop.

5

Rethinking Test Preparation

When I was a little girl, I used to kneel every night beside my third-floor bedroom window and pray that tomorrow I'd be a better person. I made long lists of the ways I would improve myself, and every night I'd hope that my prayers would be earnest enough to be heard and my performance in life would be improved. Now, I sometimes think that inside every teacher there is a child, kneeling at the window sill, praying for the strength and wisdom, energy and talent, to be more, do more, give more. Maybe we, as a profession, are so full of new resolve because every summer we have two months to think back over all that we did in the previous year and vow to improve. Maybe our lives are a perpetual self-improvement campaign because every year we get another chance to start all over again with a clean slate. I don't know. What I do know is that for my colleagues and me, it was entirely comfortable to have a checklist of areas to focus on to improve our teaching of reading.

I also know that once we had this list, we were tempted to abandon the test preparation part of our mission altogether. I think we figured that if only we could really clean up our act as teachers, if we would truly teach reading in the *most* responsible fashion imaginable, then the test scores would take care of themselves.

Probably we were also ready to give up on test preparation, concentrating only on revising our teaching of reading itself, because since we mistrusted tests and therefore we automatically mistrusted the whole notion of test preparation. Spending more time on test preparation might mean throwing more time into a bad thing.

But then we thought of Jamel. We all have stories of the Perfect Reader—the one who carries books everywhere, who devours stories with engagement and delight and intelligence—and who nevertheless scores only just above average on the tests. Jamel's problems *had* to have something to do with the tests. He clearly was a better reader than his scores indicated. We thought too of Malik, who improved steadily all year, who was reading in a predictable, steadfast fashion by April, and who nevertheless bottomed out on the tests. As we talked and thought about the Jamels and the Maliks of our lives, we knew that for these children and for others, some of the problems with the reading tests were very likely problems with the form and requirements of the tests themselves rather than problems with reading. Performing well on a reading test involves reading, yes, but it also involves a whole host of other skills and attitudes.

We also realized that reading tests will seem particularly bizarre to children who have learned to read in student-centered, literature-based classrooms. Think of it. For many other children, everyday classroom instruction often actually resembles a reading test. In these classrooms, children are frequently told what to read. They read texts others put in front of them, whether or not these texts interest them, and they generally do not come to these texts with their own purposes in mind. Instead, they are reading the texts in order to please the teacher, to perform well on the oral or written questions that accompany the text. The questions they're asked—questions such as "Where did Dick go camping?"—are the same sorts of questions children encounter on standardized reading tests. Unlike kids in our classrooms, those children receive lots of practice answering other people's short-answer questions about other people's texts.

Children in progressive classrooms, then, need an extra leg up. It certainly will be a new thing for them to be asked to read texts composed of a patchwork of disjointed passages—a factual account of a war between the red and the black ants, then a poem about an old woman in a meadow, then a narrative about three boys and a broken clock. Children from progressive, literature-based classes will have relatively little experience answering recall questions (oral or written) that ask them to recite facts from the text. Furthermore, children need to realize that a test maker isn't the nice teacher they are accustomed to working with. Test makers are trying to trick them. Children need special support in order to imagine the new kind of "author" behind this test. And so it is understandable that children from our progressive classrooms will probably need coaching in order to perform well on the unusual obstacle course of a standardized reading test.

Of course, my colleagues and I in no way advocate making reading instruction more like the tests. How sad it is to think that a majority of children in America have few opportunities to read books of their own choice for their own purposes! How sad it is to think most children do not have the opportunity to ask their own questions of a text, to generate and pursue their own lines of inquiry. How will these readers fare, I wonder, when they turn to texts for help and inspiration outside of the classroom? Clearly our goal as teachers of reading, it seems to me, must be to help children compose entire lives in which reading is a comfortable and easy process, one to turn to for assistance, for company and for dreaming. It is absolutely critical, therefore, that we teachers help our children choose books wisely by themselves, initiate their *own* ways of talking and thinking about books, and push that thinking farther and deeper. Indeed, it's our commitment to student-centered education and our willingness to do anything possible to protect our rights as teachers to teach according to our best beliefs that makes us care about standardized reading tests in the first place. So when I say that children in student-centered, literature-based reading classes will find reading tests bizarre, I'm not suggesting we alter our approach to teaching reading to more closely match the tests.

Children in progressive reading classes have lots of advantages as readers. They know what it is to compose lives as readers. They know what it is to be a part of a richly literate world. They are able to weave texts into the people and passions of their lives. They know what it is to have favorite genres, authors, times and places for reading, reading friends, and the like. They may well read more often, more fluently, with more investment, and with more skill than children in other kinds of classrooms. But at the same time, I think we need to realize that if our children are going to do as well as possible on standardized reading tests, they deserve practice and coaching in the unique challenge of performing well on those tests.

Though we were initially tempted to focus simply on improving our reading instruction so that our children would be strong readers even in ways that tests require, we soon realized that we would also need to give careful, thoughtful attention to developing wise methods of test preparation. It became clear, after some thought, that if our children's achievement on standardized tests matters to us or to them, then our children deserve to be acclimated to the genre of standardized tests. They deserve some wise instruction in its particular demands.

Our first step, then, toward rethinking test preparation was to look critically at the test preparation we and others were already doing and try to name our concerns. In most of our inquiries, this is hard to do. When we look at ideas about teaching writing or reading that have served us quite well, ideas that have been dear to our hearts, it's hard to see what's not working in those ideas. It's usually quite a challenge to develop the courage to voice our uncertainties. But criticizing our methods of test preparation was a delight, and once we began, the doubts and uncertainties rained down on us like ripe apples shaken from a tree.

As part of this process, we interviewed the teachers who are heroes within our educational community, the best reading and writing teachers we know, the teachers who host hundreds of admiring visitors and who join my colleagues and me in staffing institutes and workshops. We asked these people, "What's your curriculum for test preparation?" Surprisingly, it was as if we'd raised a question they had never even considered.

We asked, "What are the instructional methods you use to teach test preparation? How are these methods similar to and different from those you use in other parts of the school day and school curriculum?" We asked about curricular materials. "Which published materials do you rely on during test preparation? How do you choose from all that is available? Why do you particularly value the authors and philosophies of the manual, of the practice test that you use?"

The teachers we interviewed were stumped by our questions, and they joined us in being amazed by all of this. What was going on? Why were these teachers who are so very thoughtful about every other aspect of their teaching giving so little thought to their methods and curriculum for test preparation?

Partly, the problem seemed to be that none of the teachers we interviewed could recall ever having been in a study group about wise test preparation, ever having read a book on the topic, or ever having worked with mentors on the topic. Whereas they'd visited exemplary classrooms and studied the practices of effective reading and writing teachers, none of them had ever watched a pro coaching children in wise ways to take a test. They had no image of how a person could lead test preparation well and no sense of the alternative approaches or philosophies available to them.

We knew that this was partly because for a great many progressive teachers, the standardized tests are the enemy, and this means that test preparation is, too. One way of approaching test preparation is as fraught with problems as the next; one test preparation manual is as bad as the next. But just because we don't like standardized tests, it doesn't help to avert our eyes from the fact that the tests exist. We would be well-advised, instead, to give the same principled and thoughtful attention to this topic as we give to any other aspect of our curriculum.

What tended to happen during test preparation time was that the school or the district office would throw a practice test booklet and some district-generated manuals on test skills at us, and we'd throw all this at our kids. This isn't the way we would use any other published materials. If the district had given us a spelling textbook, we would have reviewed it with a discerning eye, deciding which parts to follow, when and why, and which parts to adjust or avoid. But, for many of us, standardized tests are the enemy, and this means that test preparation too is the enemy—test preparation can't be good, so why spend time thinking about it? Although we spent less time on test preparation than many of our colleagues, although some of our colleagues had different beliefs about reading and very different methods of teaching, other than this our methods for teaching children to read this unique genre were basically the same. Now, we wondered why this was true.

In thinking about it, we realized that probably we'd assumed that test preparation needed to resemble the tests. We'd assumed that the reason for test preparation was to acclimate children to the environment and conditions of a test, and therefore it seemed logical for our test preparation instruction to reflect the tone and climate of the test-taking day. Therefore, during the classroom test preparation work, our children worked as islands, with eyes on their own papers, hands to themselves, and little conversation. And for this part of our curriculum, we assumed the role of a different kind of teacher, functioning a little like the test proctors from our childhoods. We didn't think to question the fact that our test preparation work was at odds with the rest of our curriculum. Nor did we question that asking children to take one practice test after another might reinforce ineffective test-taking strategies. It's true that the conditions that exist during the testing will be somewhat at odds with the usual ones in our classrooms. That is, during the testing, children won't sit hip-to-hip reading in unison, lie in a patch of sunlight on the carpet, or work in close collaboration with each other. But none of this means that children need to study the genre of tests by sitting at their desks in rows, working alone.

We should give children a chance to experience how the tone, aura, and relationships of the classroom will change on test-taking days. Within a unit of study preparing children for standardized tests, there will come a time when it's important for children to take a practice test, or two, or three. There are reasons to sometimes give children practice like this at taking standardized tests. But, as one of our wise colleagues, Kathleen Tolan, says, "Test practice is not test preparation." Kathleen coined this phrase, and we find ourselves saying it over and over again: "Test practice is not test preparation." During test preparation, we need to teach children about this new and rather bizarre genre. We need to teach them to read for new purposes, in a new context, with new strategies. We need to draw on all that we know and believe about teaching in general and teaching reading, so that our children will learn the skills they need to do their best on standardized reading tests.

It wouldn't make sense for us to teach children to read poetry or nonfiction through one set of methods and to read standardized reading tests through a radically different set of methods. If all year long we structure our children's time in small reading groups, response groups, on-the-carpet, whole-class discussions about books, and if we teach through demonstration, one-to-one conferring, guided reading, and the like, this means we believe these are the most efficient and effective structures and methods available to us for teaching reading. Why wouldn't we then use these same structures and methods for teaching children to read standardized reading tests? If these are the ways of learning that we and this group of children have learned from and become accustomed to, then isn't it only logical that we continue to use these methods?

If our youngsters are accustomed to gathering on the carpet to read a shared, and perhaps enlarged, text together and then talking about strategies for approaching this text or for handling difficulty in this text, why wouldn't they do the same to read an excerpt from a standardized reading test? If our youngsters are accustomed to watching the strategies *we* use when we read and then trying these same strategies in their own reading, why wouldn't we model *our* methods for reading standardized tests, ask children to name what they see us doing, and then ask them to try these same strategies themselves? If conferring with individuals is a crucial part of our reading and writing workshops, if we are accustomed to observing children as they read and write, interviewing them about the strategies we see them using, then coaching them to extend or revise those strategies, why wouldn't we do the same with our youngsters as they read standardized tests?

When we marveled at how we had never really considered using our most trusted methods of teaching reading to teach children to read tests, we realized that part of the reason was that curricular development for test preparation (and it was a stretch to call what existed curricular development) resided firmly in the hands of people who hold very different beliefs about teaching reading than we hold.

Ironically, when a school or district becomes concerned about their students' levels of reading achievement, when people turn their attention to raising students' scores on the standardized reading tests, the experts they turn to are often *not* experts on the teaching of reading. Instead, the problem is identified as a test scores problem and the district turns to people who spend their lives poring over standardized tests, with their multiple-choice questions and bubbles. These people become regarded as the district's authorities on improving reading. In the name of outlining the skills students need for the reading test, these staff members end up determining the course of the district's year-long reading curriculum. Their credential for this job is that they have spent an inordinate amount of time dissecting the reading tests. We've questioned why this background entitles these people to be regarded as authorities on language arts education. Part of the problem is that the people whom many of us regard as true experts on the teaching of reading don't usually pay attention to improving standardized test scores. For a district that is under the gun to raise its scores, this can mean that these researchers and teacher-educators get ousted from their influential roles in the district. Even if this doesn't happen, the fact remains that we teachers are left unsure what our mentors would do if they were in our position.

The researchers whom we'd trust as resources on teaching reading have written about alternative forms of assessment. They have written about running records and reader interviews and portfolios and miscue analysis. These people aren't voices in the conversation about how to prepare children for standardized reading tests. Because they don't believe in standardized tests, they head down different paths. We, too, don't believe in standardized reading tests. Those of us who regard ourselves as progressive teachers of reading, who believe children should spend their time doing what good readers the world over do—reading books and talking and thinking and writing about their reading—follow in the footsteps of our mentors and drop out of the test preparation conversation. But the result is that, when it comes to test preparation, there are not different camps reflecting different beliefs about how it can be done. There is only the nonprogressive camp.

Then, too, despite the fact that school districts invest far more money in helping teachers teach test preparation well than helping them teach poetry or memoir well, teachers often feel utterly unsupported in their efforts to prepare children for the tests. "They bring us to district workshops and dole out reams of paper," teachers say, "but that isn't teaching us to prepare kids well for the tests. I've never spoken with anyone I admire who does test preparation well. I have no mentors. I have no images in my mind's eye of what teachers like me do with their children. The only help I've gotten is that the district office pushes materials at me, and I push the materials at the kids."

I know about those workshops in the district office. At one such workshop designed for third-grade teachers, the woman who was leading the workshop began by writing some cloze-type sentences on the board. The first one read

The building is tall _____ an obelisk.

    A   but
    B   red
    C   like

The instructor asked us to think about what *kind of word* was missing. I searched the answer choices. What *kinds* of words were these? I was stumped. Not by the question itself, of course—I had easily filled in the word that best fit into the blank—but I had no idea what kind of word *like* was. After some time, the instructor helped us along by suggesting it could be either a "connective" word or a "signal" word. I was completely confused, and here I was a grown-up. After explaining to us that *like* was a "connective word," the instructor gave us a list of sixteen words that were either "connective" words or "signal" words and asked us to sort them. We did our best to sort the words and as I did so, I thought about what this would be like to do as a third grader. No wonder the kids were reeling. We left the meeting with lists of skills children would need to score well on the test and lists of word categories to teach the children. The next week in those third-grade classrooms, children stopped reading books and talking about their favorite pages, about parts where the characters surprised them, and about the bits of the texts that made them angry. Now, these young readers were marking places in texts where they found "connective" and "signal" words. All over the room, children who had been excited about books, reading with each other, and talking to each other were now struggling to categorize lists of words. And all over the district, teachers were feeling frustrated. The children did not understand what they were doing.

In other districts, teachers were given guidelines for test preparation throughout the grades. In one district, a memo went out to all the teachers mandating that each school day was to begin with test preparation. First thing in the morning students would participate in a daily oral language activity designed to prepare them for the tests. The school day beginning with test preparation? Would this really improve reading scores?

Once my colleagues and I were deeply involved in a critique of our existing methods of preparing children for standardized reading tests, other issues surfaced as well. First, we wondered if we should really be teaching our upper-grade *emergent* readers the exact same test-taking strategies that we taught proficient readers. We thought, maybe it makes sense that some readers read the entire passage before answering any questions, but might it not be the case that other readers should do just the opposite? Aren't there some children who can't yet process that amount of text? With these issues and others in mind, we questioned the way in which many of us taught test takers altogether, as if there were one monolithic set of strategies that would work for everyone. Although we resist ability grouping whenever possible, we wondered whether test-taking should be taught in ability groups. At the very least, we decided we would want children to work alongside each other as they do in writing workshop, adopting, developing, trying out, refining, and practicing test-taking strategies that work for them, for a few weeks before the test each year.

Then, too, we wondered about the published materials many of us were using to support our test preparation work. Interestingly, none of the teachers we knew had selectively chosen their materials out of an array of options. Test preparation materials usually came to the classrooms in one of two ways. Either teachers dug through their old files or dusty storage cabinets in their schools for booklets that resembled the test but were often outdated, or some district office purchased test preparation materials and dropped them, as if from helicopters, into the schools. In New York City, teachers in the forty-six schools we studied each used the same test preparation booklet. Not one teacher we interviewed had questioned the choice of this particular booklet. As far as we could tell, the teachers assumed that the booklet was The Official Booklet for the Test, written by the test makers themselves. In fact, however, the New York City test was not developed by the same company that developed the test booklet we saw in hundreds of classrooms.

What's more, this particular test preparation booklet was structured somewhat differently than the New York City test. For example, in the passages of the practice book a word or two would be written in boldfaced type. One of the questions would then ask for the meaning of this boldfaced word. On the actual test, students had to find the words they were asked to define without the support of boldfaced type. Another example is that in the practice booklet, passages were often divided into numbered sections. A question might then refer to a particular section of the passage, thus providing students with support in finding the answer to the question. No such support appeared on the actual test.

As we became more and more involved in creating a curriculum for test preparation, we discovered inconsistencies between the test and the practice materials for other tests as well. It therefore seems important that teachers study closely the format of their reading tests so that they can select practice materials with great care or at least help their children to develop strategies for working with the actual test that do not rely on supports not found in it.

We were now committed to giving test taking special, closely focused attention. We knew that we wanted to be able to answer our own questions: What's your curriculum for test preparation? Which methods and materials do you use? It was easy for us to say what we *would not* want to do: we didn't want to turn over control of the curriculum to others, we didn't want to reflexively teach our own students as we had been taught, and we didn't want to throw handfuls of test-taking tips at the children in a flurry. It was also easy for us to say what we probably *would* want to do: we wanted to use the same methods and structures that we use in our best teaching of reading and writing. Now, it was time to take our ideas into classrooms.

6

Reading the Test Passages

It's reading workshop time. The children in the classroom I'm visiting are absorbed in their books. Some are reading shoulder-to-shoulder in partnerships, stopping every fifteen minutes to retell their books to each other; others read alone. Daniel catches the teacher's eye. He has just finished *The Cay,* snapping the book shut. The teacher pulls her chair up alongside his. "Finished!" he says, ready to return the book to the class library. "It was pretty good, too."

She gestures for him to stay. "Daniel," she asks, "what do you usually do when you finish a book?"

Daniel looks mystified. Wasn't the answer obvious? "I get a new one."

"The reason I asked, Daniel, is that for me, finishing a book is like reaching the top of a mountain. When I get to the end, I don't just turn around and race down the mountain. I like to stay there, at the top, and look back over where I've come. I like to linger at the end a bit and to look back at the whole view. Why don't you linger at the end of *The Cay* and look at the whole view for a while." She and Daniel talked over what he might do, and then he headed off to reread favorite sections, in light of understanding the whole book.

Two days later, as the students gathered on the carpet to hear the last pages of our read-aloud book, *The Maestro,* Daniel explained some ways we could think back and make more of the whole of the book. Soon, small groups of children, each with its own copy of the book, were trying different ways to think more about it.

This sort of work, developing habits of mind and strategies, constitutes an important part of the reading instruction in the classrooms my colleagues and I know best. As we began to help teachers imagine new possibilities for teaching youngsters to read standardized reading tests, we knew that in similar ways we'd now want to coach and demonstrate strategies we thought might be especially helpful for children to use during standardized reading tests. We hoped that in some ways the tone and texture of test preparation teaching would feel similar to that of our reading instruction, but we also knew that in other ways the test preparation work would inevitably feel different, because within a study of reading tests children wouldn't be pursuing their own independent goals and projects, as they do in an independent reading workshop. Our testing minilessons would not be able to lift the level of ongoing work, as they do in reading and writing workshops. They would need to gear children up for the test preparation work in the first place. That is, within a test preparation unit, minilessons would have to organize and initiate each day's efforts.

We knew that just as Daniel's teacher had coached him on strategies he could use as he finished *The Cay*, we would now coach children as they read standardized reading tests. Just as the strategies invented in one-on-one conferences became whole-class minilessons in our reading workshops, so, too, would this happen in our test preparation work. We knew the source of the minilessons, then, but we didn't know their content, that is, we didn't know what strategies might help our kids do better on tests.

Our inquiry was complicated by the fact that we weren't working with only one form of test. Across our region and across the country, children take a variety of reading tests: multiple-choice, short-answer, and even extensive writing. Typically, though, the tests require the children to read passages and answer the questions that follow. Some tests also have grammar and spelling sections. A common format is the cloze test, passages with blanks in place of some words. In cloze tests, kids are required to fill in the correct word from four possibilities. These types of reading tests are more fully explored in Chapter 7.

We decided to begin our study by investigating the strategies children use while taking tests that require them to read passages and answer questions about them. In order to learn strategies that might help children, we decided to take the exams ourselves.

Research Ourselves and
Our Students as Test Takers

About thirty of us gathered around a big table feeling clamminess come out on our palms. As we waited for the fifth-grade reading test to be passed out, people made jokes about failing. Not everyone was laughing. At the same time, the half of the group assigned to research the test takers was not at ease either. When someone takes a reading test, what's there to see? An hour later, after we'd taken a segment of the test and then shared, revisited, and compared notes, our heads were spinning. How could we have waited so many years to do this?

When our little experiment was over, the feeling that swept the room was, "Wow, these tests are tricky! No wonder my kids don't find them easy." We were conscious, too, that the tricks of the test didn't feel like they were based on how well a person reads. We knew we'd need to study this some more, and we suspected it would be unbelievably powerful to have our students' parents try what we'd just tried so they, too, could understand how it feels to take tests such as these. We also talked about how funny it was that we were proud of ourselves for surviving this fifth-grade test. A few of us spoke about taking the Graduate Record Exam next time, a test designed for college graduates. Others were very, very quiet during this discussion. Later, thinking about the conversation, I realized that among this group of very intelligent teachers there were people who had scored well on standardized tests and people who hadn't. In our professional community, we often look at ourselves as skilled readers and make generalizations about what skilled readers tend to do, but the truth is, we are not all skilled test takers. We can't all mine our experiences in order to talk about what skilled test takers tend to do. As will be true of almost any group, some of us excelled at tests whereas others found the fifth-grade test intimidating enough that the idea of taking the GRE was not at all appealing.

We never did take the GRE together.

Even without taking an adult exam, however, we were able to talk about what strategies we'd used to read the passages and to answer the questions on this fifth-grade test. What startled us was that, as test takers, we were very different from each other.

Drew approached the test deliberately, cautiously covering each bit of ground, leaving no stone unturned. He first read the directions. Then he read the sample question. Then he read all the sample answers. He turned to the first passage on the test and read it through slowly. "I'm trying to envision the story, I want to hold it all in my mind," he said. Then he read question number one and each possible answer. Only after reading each possible answer did he select the one he thought was best. At this point, he returned with his usual thoroughness to reread all the possible answers, justifying each rejection or acceptance in order to check himself. If a question called for specifics, he looked back at the text and reread the passage from start to finish rather than just rereading the pertinent section. "I missed this answer," he explained. "I might have missed something else too. I want to be on solid ground."

Others approached the test with none of Drew's caution and conscientiousness. Anya, for example, headed directly for the questions, for a time bypassing the directions and the passage altogether. She skimmed over several questions, then said, "I think I get what they want." Looking back to the passage, she read it over quickly with an eye to finding the answers. As she found an answer, she filled in her answer sheet accordingly. Once she found the answer she wanted, she rarely glanced at other possible answers. She read all the possibilities carefully only when the answer she had expected wasn't in the list of options.

Drew and Anya weren't isolated extremes. About a third of us approached the test in a manner that resembled Drew's approach. Others of us were more like Anya. Although those of us who were like Anya didn't all bypass the passage and directions to first read the questions, we did not read the text and then the questions from head to toe as if they were a book. Our eyes flickered between text and questions. More strikingly, we didn't think of what we did during the test as being similar to normal reading. "It's more like solving puzzles," Laurie said. "It's like a game, a contest. When I take a test, I'm trying to score, to win. I'm not settling in for a nice comfortable read."

The variety of ways in which we approached the test startled us. Most of us felt as if we'd never made a choice about the way we took tests. We took tests in the only way we could imagine. Now, faced with the differences in our methods, we had questions. Were some strategies better than others, or were the differences immaterial, simply a quirk of personality?

It soon became clear that, at least within our community, the people who identified themselves as good test takers approached the test more like Anya did, and the people who regarded themselves as poor test takers approached the test more like Drew did. But should we conclude that the way Anya approached the test was more effective than the way Drew approached it? Should everyone try to take on some of Anya's strategies?

We can't pretend to have any definitive answers. The differences between Drew and Anya are no doubt partly attributable to personality differences, and their previous test-taking success or lack of it has no doubt given them differing levels of confidence as test takers. However, we concluded that Anya's strategies probably did feed into and support her skills as a test taker.

Others will want to do as we did—take tests ourselves, notice differences in the group's strategies, and decide whether any of the differences suggest an agenda for instruction. You will also need to watch children in your classroom to see if they can be separated into different kinds of test takers. Within our community, we concluded that it would probably be helpful for Drew and others like him to try to take on more of the attitudes and approaches that Anya used.

We asked teachers to identify for us their star achievers on the reading tests. We wanted to see if these test takers were alike, one to the next, and we wanted to see if they were more like Anya than like Drew. Jared, a fifth grader at the Bronx New School, was the first child I interviewed and observed. "For me, taking a reading test is *nothing* like reading a book," he said. "When I read a book, reading just flows. I take my time, and I let thoughts and ideas just come to me. I don't really stop and do any work. I just flow through the pages letting my mind get ideas. But in the test, it's completely different. I am trying to think of specific things they want me to know. I'll do whatever it takes to figure out what they want from me."

After interviewing Jared, I watched him reading a Gary Paulsen book. He lay on a pillow on a corner of the carpet. He first glanced back over the pages he'd already read, then settled into the story.

Stretched out on his back on the floor, his knees crossed, he began reading quickly and with no pauses, no breaks in his attention.

Twenty minutes later, Jared and his class were given a practice test and told to find themselves a comfortable place in the room. Jared could go anywhere. He chose to sit at a desk, his back to the class. He sat erect in the chair, gripping his pencil even as he began to read. He read a bit of the passage, then he bubbled in the answer to the third question. "I nailed that one," he commented. Watching him, it seemed to me that he had found the right phrase to describe what he was doing. He was nailing those little questions. He was homing in on the answers. "It's sort of like a video game," he said. "I'm going, 'Gotcha!' in my mind. 'Bing!' One answer. 'Bang!' Another one. 'Gotcha!'"

Over the next few weeks, we interviewed and watched other skilled test takers and found that almost without fail they tended to move fluidly from the text to the questions, then back to the text. Many began by reading the questions, but even those who didn't read with an awareness that the purpose for this reading was to answer questions that were coming soon. The skilled test takers thought and talked more about what "they" (the test makers) would probably ask. They read the passage noting dates or facts, thinking, *"They'll* probably ask about that." They were apt to notice a weird phrase and think, "I'm going to remember where this is. There might be a question on it." They read with an audience and a purpose in mind. The audience was the scorer—the judge—and the purpose was to find the answer that was on the answer sheet. Skilled test takers read with a judge perched on their shoulder, and the judge has only one right answer in mind for each question.

In a reading workshop these same children read very differently. In that context, they might look up from a book to say, "This is a boring story" or "This is like when I go to my grandmother's house." But while taking a test, the star test takers don't seem to expect that the test will be interesting or that it will relate to their own lives. Whereas less-skilled test takers might read a passage from the test and say, "I disagree with this," or talk about how they wouldn't do what a character in the passage did, the skilled test takers did very little of this. Watching, my colleagues and I decided that it is a problem when children respond to test passages in the same way that they respond to novels they've chosen to read for pleasure. The responses we hope readers have to books in their lives are often not helpful when taking a reading test. Jared's goal wasn't to enjoy or relate to a story, it was to score well on a series of questions, and we thought his attitude was exemplary.

It was beginning to be clear to us that there was something unique and useful about the way that Jared and Anya read tests. We wanted this for most of our test takers. We weren't brashly confident of this; we still had questions. We were particularly unclear about whether Jared and Anya's approach would work for struggling readers who were already swamped by the tests, who had trouble just comprehending the passage, and who might get derailed by any agenda other than the one of somehow making sense of the passage. We still planned to progress tentatively, watching to see if our efforts to teach kids strategies might do certain kids more harm than good. Nonetheless, we decided we did now have at least a general sense of a strategy we might teach that could perhaps dramatically help children become better readers of the passages on their reading tests.

Intervene in a Responsible Way

Before describing strategies and methods, let me double back on our trail of thought to address the insecurities we felt about intervening. Let me also address the insecurity I now feel about putting our teaching interventions onto the page for readers.

The truth is that intervening to teach anybody anything can be a frightening undertaking. José has written a draft summarizing four things he did on his summer vacation. We listen and say, "José, of all that you've written about, what's the *one* thing you're most interested in?" Soon we've got José with a blank sheet of paper in front of him, this one bearing the specific title, "Basketball in the Park" instead of "My Summer Vacation." Will our advice help him, or will it make him more resistant? Will we shake his confidence, or equip him with new skills?

We, as José's teachers, feel fairly confident of our intervention in such a case. Our confidence may come because someone once asked us in a similar way to focus our writing, and it helped. Our

confidence may also come from reading and hearing about countless other teachers who have coached young writers in similar
ways, helping youngsters find their focus. Also, we know in the
long run, if José narrows his topics in this manner, this will probably work for him as a writer. But if José's writing were going to be
scored that day, we would have a hard time feeling confident that
our intervention would necessarily yield a higher score. José might
very well be stymied and discouraged or sullen about the fact that
we've essentially made him start all over. He may feel like he has
almost nothing to say about basketball in the park. Our intervention may or may not lead to *instant* improvement.

It is always scary to teach in active, assertive ways. Even with
José, many teachers would not have intervened in such a forceful
way, preferring instead to simply chat with him about his topic—
the summer vacation—and then perhaps saying, "It sounds great!
Keep going" or "José, why don't you add all that you've told me?"
These supportive comments are nice, but if this sort of comment is
the only help José ever receives on his writing, he'll be missing out
on important lessons. For this reason, my colleagues and I in the
Teachers College Reading and Writing Project often urge teachers
to have the courage to be clear, assertive teachers. "We can't be
afraid to make a difference," we say.

It is probably the case, however, that if we are timid about intervening in ways that affect how a child goes about writing, we'll be
a hundred times more reluctant to intervene in ways that affect
how a child goes about taking standardized reading tests. When
we intervene in the writing workshop, we can rely on the stories of
countless other teachers who've done the same. We're not breaking
new trails. Our shelves are full of books on the teaching of writing,
which tell story after story of other teachers who've pulled their
chairs alongside children who, like José, held a draft that resembled a list. We can read what these other teachers said and did.
Fortunately, and unfortunately, our shelves are not also full of
books about teachers who have coached children as they learn to
read standardized tests. When we watch and listen to children taking standardized tests, therefore, we learn things no one will have
forewarned us about. We break new trails. The onus is on us to
invent wise teaching in response to what we see. Then, too, the

pressure is on us to be certain that our interventions yield higher scores. When we coach young writers, our interventions needn't instantly yield better results on that day's piece of writing or even on that week's piece of writing. It's enough for us to sense that in the long run our advice to José will probably bear fruit. But when the goal is to improve children's scores on reading tests, we look for instant and concrete success.

In this chapter and in the chapters that follow, I describe ways in which we have intervened in hopes of lifting the scores and widening the repertoire of strategies children use when they read standardized tests. I suspect that our readers will eye these strategies with a skeptical eye, asking, "Is it *truly* the case that this suggested strategy is an effective one?" It is reasonable to ask this question. The stakes are high. There aren't professional test takers (as there are professional writers) who can demonstrate for us the methods they use. The truth is, there are no strategies for taking tests that will always yield higher scores, and certainly there are no strategies for taking tests that will make all our children perform as we would wish. I am, then, simply sharing the best ideas we have right now and inviting readers to try these on for size, to weigh them against all you see and believe. The ideas are far from definitive. But my colleagues and I are definite in our belief that, as teachers, we need to gather our courage and not be afraid to teach.

In Chapter 5, I mentioned the story of how we asked teachers we especially admired to tell us about their curriculum for test preparation: "What comes first for you?" "What seems essential to you, what is fundamental for you?" Eventually, we asked these questions of ourselves. When teaching children to read passages on standardized reading tests, what seems paramount? Our answer was that it seemed important to help children realize that this kind of reading was basically different than the reading Jared did as he lay on the carpet with a pillow, flowing along through the plot line of his Gary Paulsen book. We decided it was important to help children read in a sit-up, take-hold-of-the-pencil, "find-out-what-*they*-want" kind of way. We knew that no instruction would transform Drew's timidity and conscientiousness into Anya's confidence, but we had a hunch that we could help test takers like Drew be more efficient and aggressive as test takers and more prepared for the questions they'd face. We knew we wanted to help all our children to read the passages with an awareness that the purpose for this reading was to answer the questions.

We later learned that people in commercial test preparation programs around the country also believe this is helpful. My colleagues and I weren't certain how to help children read the test passages as if this was a video game they wanted to ace rather than a novel they wanted to enjoy. We thought, however, that it might be helpful for children to read the questions first and only then turn to the passages.

In order to explore whether our hunch would, in fact, yield better test-taking strategies and better scores, we gathered a small group of children and gave them a minilesson. "You may want to try a strategy I use when I take a test," I said to them. "Even though the directions say read the passage first and then answer the questions, I often go straight to the questions. I first read the questions and I think a lot about them." Then I added, "The questions often give me an idea of what the passage will be about. Would you try this? Work with a partner. Read the questions first, then think about the questions together. What might the passage be about, if these are the questions?" Then we divided ourselves up and each cluster of us watched a pair of children.

Chantell skipped past the page-long passage and went directly to the question, "Who didn't want the children to play with ants?" Talking with her partner, she spun out a possible story.

"I think the kids; the kids, they are on a picnic. They are on a picnic and they open their lunch bag and ants are in it! So the kid takes an ant and puts it in the other kid's pants!" Soon Chantell's partner was joining in and together they spun out a glorious, funny, enticing story about children with ants in their pants. Finally, they turned to the second question. It didn't exactly fit with their children-on-a-picnic-with-ants-in-their-pants story, but with some finesse they extended their story so as to connect the dots, making the first and the second questions scaffold a tale. Soon there was a mother in their imagined story who didn't want her kids to get dirty, and the story went on and on.

Finally, the children finished following my directions, reading the questions and thinking about how the passage would probably go. Now they turned to read the actual passage. Imagine the chaos as they encountered an utterly different story and had to undo the story they had spun to take in the new, actual story! Their home-made story with kids on a picnic with ants in their pants and a mother who didn't want anyone to get dirty was far more alluring than the actual story, and in the end, the girls combined what they had already imagined with what was on the page, thus creating a huge tangle.

What a lesson this was for me and my colleagues! We'd spent a great deal of time thinking about our very best minilesson. We'd relied on the expertise of about fifteen experienced teachers and two researchers from Educational Testing Service to invent this minilesson. Despite our combined efforts, our minilesson made a giant mess of our children's test taking.

Properly humbled, we reminded ourselves of the wise words of Maimonides, "I have learned much from my teachers but more from my students." We thanked our lucky stars that we'd watched closely to see the results of our intervention, and we promised our-selves to never, ever leave out that step.

Strategies for Reading the Test Passages

Back at the drawing board, we thought over what had gone wrong in our minilesson and prepared ourselves for a second try. This time, we gathered together a whole class of children.

"Kids," Kathleen Tolan said, "I've been thinking about what it's like for me when I take a reading test. For me, it is like a scav-enger hunt. Do you know how scavenger hunts go? Everyone gets a list of things to find—a pink rock, a flower with at least six petals—and then everyone has to go and find those things. Well, when I take a reading test, it's a little like I'm going on a scaven-ger hunt. Only the list of things I'm supposed to find is the list of questions at the end of the passage. So let me show you what I do when I take a test." Then, using an overhead projector, Kathleen enlarged one page from a test preparation booklet. The page began with a short passage and ended with multiple-choice ques-tions. The first question was, "Why was Bark a special dog?" Reading the question, Kathleen mused, "Okay, so that is the first thing on my list. I'm going to be looking for reasons why the dog is special." Then, she read the next question, "How old was Mr. Mishima?" She again made a note to look for this piece of information. She continued until she'd scanned four of the six questions, and then she said, "That's enough for me to remember. I'm going to start reading the passage now." The kids watched as she began to read. For demonstration purposes, Kathleen read aloud, although she was clearly reading aloud to herself, not to the listeners. Early in her reading she ran into a piece of information that answered one of the questions. "There it is! That's the answer," she said, and immediately registered the correct answer on the answer sheet.

It wasn't surprising, of course, that this strategy worked for her. After all, she is a grownup and a teacher, taking a fourth-grade reading test. My colleagues and I had learned from our previous attempt not to be overly confident that strategies that seemed logical and worked for us would necessarily work for kids. We fanned out among the kids to watch what happened when children first read the questions, gathering a list of items to find in the passage.

This time, the transformation was remarkable and very exciting. It felt as if throughout the room, children were leaning forward over their papers yelping "Got it!" or "There it is!" They moved often between the passages and the questions. None of the children seemed to be passively going for a ride through the text.

A new problem surfaced, however. As children read the passages, they found answers to questions out of sequential order. A child might first find the answer to the third question (which might be listed as number nine because the question numbers do not begin afresh with each new passage). Next the child might find the answer to the first question after the passage, numbered seven. For students taking tests where answers are recorded directly in the test booklet, skipping around while answering questions raised the possibility that students might miss some questions. If we were going to encourage students to answer out of order, we knew we needed to teach them to scan each page and ensure that each answer was filled in before turning to the next page.

An even greater problem arose for students taking tests in which answers were recorded on bubble sheets. When children moved between the exam and the answer sheet and didn't progress sequentially, answering number nine, then number seven, there was an increased likelihood that they'd get disoriented and end up darkening in the wrong bubbles. We had briefly considered forgoing the advice to read the questions first. In every other way, however, this advice seemed to have been very helpful for most children. Instead of taking back this advice, we set out to find a solution to the possibility of confusion on the answer sheet. Most of us, in the end, decided to suggest that as children read the passage and encountered answers, they should fill in the answers on the exam booklet itself, under the question. This avoided any confusion. Then, after the children had read the entire passage, and made sure all the questions were answered, they could turn to their answer sheet to fill in all the bubbles for that passage.

Technically, of course, this process goes against the directions in several ways. First, the directions on the tests our children were taking stated they were to first read the passage and only then the questions. Second, the directions told the children they were not to write on the test booklet. We talked about this with many teachers and with Ted Chittenden and Jacqueline Jones of Educational Testing Service. Everyone felt confident that there had never been any negative consequences for the children who *do* write on the test booklets, but, of course, there may be places where children could conceivably be penalized for breaking this rule. This issue is worth investigating. In every instance we know about, the test booklets aren't reused, and even if they were, there aren't many teachers among us who wouldn't spring for the small cost of new booklets if this would allow our children to do better on tests. Ted and Jacqueline suggested that, in fact, the instruction not to write on the test booklets might have been written for the express purpose of making it less likely that all children will do well on standardized tests. As we said in Chapter 2, the purpose of a norm-referenced test is to separate kids, one from the next, and telling children not to write on the test booklet can keep kids from doing all sorts of things which conceivably might help them. The instruction not to write on the test booklets might possibly exist to handicap some kids, so that they can be divided into good or less good scorers.

As we looked at the tests, we knew there were several subjects we needed to discuss with the kids to help them develop a things-I-need-to-look-for list as they read the test passages. We know that for some tests, such as the Michigan Educational Assessment Program (MEAP) test, which is composed of two very long passages each followed by a long set of questions, we would need to think about how many questions each of us could remember while reading a passage. Some kids found they could effectively keep three questions in their heads as they read. For other children, it was enough to have two at a time in mind. This meant they would only read two questions and put two items on their list of things to search for before they began reading the passage. Having only two items on the list may not seem very helpful, but the strategy's contribution is not only that readers have this list of items to find but also that readers take on a new stance. Even a list of two things to look for can help readers to read the passage as a test rather than as a novel.

As we watched children reading the questions first, we saw that when they paused midway through reading to circle an answer in their test booklet, many lost their place in the passage. They needed ways to quickly find their place again and to read on. We helped children learn to make a mark in the passage where they left off reading. Others realized that once they'd interrupted themselves in the midst of the passage, it was helpful to resume by "backing up," so they actually reread a few lines of the passage before continuing. This made it less necessary for them to identify the exact place where they left off, and it also allowed them some time to regain hold on the story line of the passage.

Over time, by observing youngsters as they read the standardized tests and by actually recalling what we did when we read those passages, we eventually developed a repertoire of strategies to be used by test takers. We noticed, for example, that when we adults read the passages, many of us made mental notes of facts and definitions that we expect might later be included in a question. Among the children we observed, it was only the most skilled test takers who seemed to do this. We gathered children again, and Kathleen used an overhead projector to enlarge a passage from a practice test. "Would you all be researchers and watch what I do when I read," she said. After she'd read a few questions and developed her list of things to look for, she read a line or two of the passage, pausing to underline the date when the story took place and the age of the grandmother. Each time she underlined one of these facts, she muttered to herself, "They'll probably ask about this" or "Now I can come back to this fact if they want it."

After a few minutes, she paused. "So what do you notice me doing?" she asked, and the class talked about her underlining. The discussion was heated. "You're cheating!" one child said. Others agreed. "You can't write on the test," they all said.

I have discussed earlier our views on this subject, but the children in this class had been well-indoctrinated into "the law" about not writing on test booklets. Some teachers might deemphasize that rule. Or, if the teacher and the children are law-abiding enough that writing on the test booklets feels wrong, children could underline key facts on their practice tests in order to learn to make mental notes with pretend underlining when they take actual tests. However it is done, learning how to pack the brain with information that might come up in the questions is an important skill, especially if the test has a listening comprehension section. The goal is to energize children to read with an "I'm going to pack this fact into my brain because they might ask me about it" mentality.

In one class, the focus on packing information into the brain gave rise to another issue. Although students were reading anticipating the questions, after they had answered them they never went back to the passage for confirmation. It was as if they were testing their own ability to remember. In fact, when we asked them how they chose a particular answer, they often explained that they remembered it from the story. We told the children that test makers sometimes try to trick them and try to trick their memory. For example, one test contained a passage about two children playing a game. The question asked the student to pick the word that best described how the boy felt *at the beginning* of the game. The choices were "(A) bored, (B) afraid, (C) confused, (D) excited." Just relying on memory, a student might choose (B) because in the story the boy was said to have felt afraid. At the very beginning of the story, however, the boy gave a bored yawn, so (A) would be the right answer. This is a typical trick on tests, and many students fall for it because instead of going back to the passage they rely on their memories.

Once we had convinced students of the need to go back to the text to confirm their answers, we discovered that we needed to teach them *how* to go back. Very often, students embarked on a time-consuming search for answers by rereading the entire passage, starting from the first word and moving to the last. It was as if they had no map of the passages in mind, no sense of the parts of the passage where they might find a certain kind of information. We decided to teach these students that they could simply jot key words, or summary words, in the margins of their tests, alongside the paragraphs. These words would serve as reminders to them of the content of each paragraph. *Kitten* might mean that's the paragraph where the character got a kitten for her birthday. *Sick* could remind a reader that in this paragraph the cat needed to go to the veterinarian. With key words as markers, children are less apt to reread whole passages looking for answers. Of course, for some children, the act of deciding on a key or summary word is too exhausting and too distracting to be useful.

As children began to use some of these strategies for reading the tests, we could see that some were still feeling overwhelmed by the passages. For them, the amount of text on each page was just too much. When we conferred with them, these students spoke of how their eyes got tired and how the words felt all squashed together. We began offering those students some strategies for managing the difficulties they were having keeping their eyes on the text. For some, we suggested they cover up some of the text with an index card while reading to make the text seem less overwhelming.

We realized some passages were difficult to read just because of the way they looked on the page. The print was dense, and this intimidated some children. To respond to this problem, Kathleen Tolan gathered a group of her students who were having particular difficulty dealing with the density of the text. The children watched as Kathleen took *Owl Moon*, a picture book they had read, reread, and fallen in love with, and began retyping it so that it looked like a test passage. She typed it in a small font, with very little space between the lines and words, and she crammed it all on one page. She then pointed out to the kids that just because a story looked too difficult, didn't mean it was too difficult. Then she took out a folder filled with the typed texts of some of the kids' favorite picture books. She asked the kids to reread these versions of the books in order to get used to reading texts that looked like those they would encounter on the tests. (It is important to note here that

I am not advocating using children's literature to teach test preparation. In the next chapter, I discuss some reasons why it's important to separate children's literature from test preparation. Kathleen simply wanted her students to see that sometimes what made a text difficult was only how it looked on the page.)

Some students had no difficulty with the size and density of the print but had trouble jumping from one passage to a completely different one. Often these students would struggle to keep each passage separate in their minds. They would sometimes mix the contents together, and this would confuse them as they tried to answer the questions. "Was that boy a liar in *this* story, or was it in the story before? Is the parrot from eastern Africa, or was that where the locomotive went?" they would ask themselves. We suggested these students take a very short break in between passages, giving their eyes and brains time to rest. Karen discovered that if she looked out the window for a minute, that would help. Javier began to stretch his arms and legs between passages. The kids invented their own ways to erase one passage from mind before reading the next one.

In some tests, however, the last section of the test might refer to a passage at the beginning of the test. For example, on the MEAP test, the writing section might ask the student to write about a story she had read at the beginning of the test. Of course, in these instances, students would have to make a big effort to *keep* the passages in mind. Instead of trying to wipe the slate clear, they tried to hold onto every part of every passage in case there was a question about it later, when they couldn't check back. For a number of students, this proved difficult because the plot lines of the different passages would get tangled together. For them, we suggested that instead of trying to keep all the bits of the test in mind, they should just rescan the earlier passages on the test to remind themselves of what they were about before turning to the writing section of the test.

Our main goal in teaching kids to read test passages, then, was to help them develop a mind-set for taking tests that was different from the one they'd developed for everyday reading. To do this, we studied children as they struggled through practice tests and as they took pieces of our advice. As problems became apparent, we would try to design minilessons to resolve or prevent them. Over time, after working in many classrooms, we developed a repertoire of minilessons that seemed to be useful for many kids, much of the time. This repertoire included

- helping kids develop a scavenger-hunt-type list of things to look for as they read the passages by having them read the questions first
- teaching kids to find out how many questions they can hold in their minds as they read the passages
- showing them how to fill in all the answers on each test booklet page before filling in the corresponding bubbles on the answer sheet
- teaching kids ways to mark the passage in order to make it easier to go back to find or check specific parts—these include writing key words in the margins and circling or underlining "landmark" words or phrases
- showing kids how to use an index card to block out distracting print or to act as a placeholder
- retyping familiar or easy text to look as daunting and dense as the test passages to give kids confidence and experience in reading in the test format

Of course, this is only a starting point. As teachers work with their own students and their own tests, they will inevitably develop a unique and more extensive repertoire of strategies for helping students to read test passages.

7

Navigating the Formats of Tests

Just like oil and water, *Charlotte's Web* and standardized tests don't mix. We believe in learning to read good literature. We believe in learning to do well on tests. But we don't believe the two kinds of learning are the same. The reading on standardized reading tests is very different from any other kind of reading. The type of thinking a reader does when he gets lost in the world of a story should be different than the thinking he does when he tries to figure out the answer to a test maker's question. Kelly, a fourth grader, explained the difference to us: When she reads a novel or her comic books, she curls up in bed and pretends that she's the characters in the story, imagining herself going on their adventures, fighting their fights. But when she takes a reading test, it's like taking a math quiz. She sits up straight, holds tight to her pencil, and keeps her mind on the questions.

It's not just that the experiences of reading for pleasure and reading for a test are different; the materials are also very different. Test preparation should be taught with materials that look like the test. In the same way that we would not use a magazine article to teach poetry, but would use poetry to teach poetry, we also need to use test practice materials to prepare kids for tests.

Know the Format of the Reading Test

Most of us have learned the wisdom of the Boy Scout motto, "Be Prepared." If we're expected to deliver a speech in a new setting, we arrive early to look over the place, to get our bearings. If we're expected to arrive at a new place exactly on time, we swing past the appointed spot a day earlier, rehearsing the trip. Unfortunately, the reading tests our students take come so cloaked in secrecy that it is hard for any of us to follow that wise advice and be prepared.

It is startling, in fact, how ignorant most of us are about the tests that now control so much of our destinies and our students' destinies. During the past two years, our study of tests led us to interview teachers and principals across the country. Time and again we found that people don't know much about the design and format of the tests their students take, and know even less about how their particular test stacks up against other tests. "I really only catch a fleeting glimpse of our tests," one teacher told us. "They are kept under lock and key until test day. Then as children complete the tests, they are whisked out of sight. We get the scores back, but never the tests themselves."

It's not too surprising that if we, as teachers, feel uncertain about the format and design of our reading tests, our students do as well. And yet, surely, test preparation work needs to orient children to the particulars of this new format for reading. In order to design a test preparation program that could do just that, my colleagues and I gathered together whatever tests we could find (or whatever test preparation materials we could find) and began reading them with excruciating care.

We learned that reading tests tend to come in one of several formats. One type of test is composed of short passages written in a variety of genres, followed by questions about the content of the passages. For example, questions such as, "How did the father feel at the end of the story?" "Which of the following is NOT true according to the passage?" "What year was the light bulb invented?"

Another test format includes fewer and longer passages, followed by questions. In one such test, about two thirds of the questions related to the content of the passage and the remaining third asked students about literary terminology, syntax, and literature. For example, questions may resemble this:

The author began this story with:

   A   a description of the character
   B   dialogue
   C   the resolution
   D   the conflict

Where would you be most likely to find this passage?

A   an encyclopedia
B   a magazine
C   a novel
D   a dictionary

Questions might also be about grammar, for example, "Which of these is the simple subject of the following sentence?"

Some reading tests consist solely of cloze-type passages, followed by four fill-in choices. Often, the passages on these tests are solely nonfiction.

Yet another type of test combines all these formats: a reading comprehension section with questions related to the content of the passages; a section that asking students to choose the correct spelling of a word from a list of choices; a section asking them to choose a synonym from a list of possibilities; a section requiring them to listen to a passage and answer questions about it; and sometimes a part where students respond in writing to the passages and work on editing.

This variety of reading test formats amazed us. We hadn't expected that the formats and expectations for different tests would vary as much as they do. As we learned about the formats and expectations of the tests, we began to wonder what would be the important things to teach children about them. We decided that each of us would take our questions into a classroom and watch children as they tried to navigate through the tests.

When I arrived in a fifth-grade classroom in Missouri, students were scattered around the room with copies of practice Terra Nova tests. *Terra Nova* literally means "new ground." This is a McGraw-Hill test, as are the Comprehensive Test of Basic Skills (CTBS) and the California Test Bureau (CTB). But unlike those two tests, the Terra Nova claims to break new ground because it contains some elements of a performance test.

First, I saw Tony skip the first page of the test. "I always skip that," he said. "It's the directions, I know what it's going to say, so I don't need to read it." In fact, the statement he skipped was a kind of orientation statement, an opening or summary for the passage to follow, and this introductory statement pointed the way to an answer for one of the ensuing questions. But even if the statement had turned out to be a routine starting direction, it would have been essential to read it, for otherwise how could one know?

Across the room, Angel was leaving bubble after bubble blank. "I'm not sure what the answers are, and I don't want to get them wrong," he explained. If Angel had known that every blank set of answers would automatically be marked wrong by the test graders, and that even random guesses might have yielded a higher test score, he certainly would have filled in a choice for every question.

Shawna was pausing for a long time over one question. She explained, "I can't remember yet which thing happened first, but I'm not looking!" She, as well as other students, had thought that to look back at the story for answers was not allowed, or not in good taste, or at least not what a good test taker would do. "It's testing what you remember," she explained, "so you're not supposed to look back." If she had known that checking back was part of doing well, she undoubtedly would have done it.

At the other side of the room, Stephen sat and didn't seem to be working on the test any longer. When I asked him what he was thinking, he replied, "There are too many stories. I'm confused. I can't do it." He was feeling the muddle of working on a test made of up many different passages strung together. He was confused, as any of us would be, being tugged back and forth among different stories. He needed to get used to keeping all the stories separate in his mind so he wouldn't get frustrated.

When my colleagues and I met the following week to discuss what we had found, we discovered that wherever we looked, no matter what the class, no matter what the test, children had difficulties that would dissolve if they were to learn more about the format of the test. Each of us told stories of children who skipped the directions, who left blanks when they were unsure of answers, who wrongly believed that they would be cheating if they looked back at the passage or at other parts of the test. Children also had problems with format issues that were related to the specific test they were taking. We came to realize that just as teachers needed to become familiar with the format of the tests their students were taking, so, too, the children needed to get to know the tests very well in order to avoid certain pitfalls.

Orient Your Students to the Test

In our study group we had agreed that children needed to learn more about the format of reading tests before taking them. But we knew that simply telling them thirty things about the format of the test wouldn't be teaching in the best ways we know. First of all, the knowledge probably wouldn't stick. Furthermore, even if the children could learn about the format of the test that way, knowing a list of thirty facts would only be useful to them on one particular test. To learn how to be a better test taker overall, a student would need to learn how to find for herself the list of thirty facts to know. She should learn how to look over a test to see how she should approach it: What kinds of questions are there? Should I guess when I don't know? What kind of passages are there? Without learning how to orient herself to the tests she will take all her life, the student will only be an improved test taker when there is a teacher there to feed her details about the format she needs to know. In the Teachers College Reading and Writing Project community, educators believe that students learn more, and learn more deeply, when they are involved in the process of discovering the knowledge. So, just as they do in reading and writing workshops, teachers who saw areas where kids needed help began units of study on these issues. When kids were confused by the test format, the teachers began to study the topic with the students, bringing the whole class into any inquiry.

Katherine Bomer began this work in her classroom by passing out copies of texts from different genres—plays, short stories, atlases, telephone books, and newspaper articles. "Let's talk about what we know about the format of these different types of texts that helps us to handle them well," she said. The kids began to browse through the materials.

"I know the phone book is in alphabetical order," said one.

"I know how to read a play because I know you don't read aloud the parts in italics or the names; those parts are so you know what's going on and who's talking," said another.

"I know in a newspaper article that the important things come first and the details come after, getting smaller until the end."

They discussed how their knowledge of the format of each kind of material helped them to read it better. After this discussion, Katherine handed them each a practice reading test. "What can we find out that can help us read this better?" she asked. And in their response groups that day, and for the rest of the week, they tried to find out about the format of the test, and to invent ways to make that knowledge work to their advantage.

Dan Fellman helped his students begin their study in a different way. His class had just finished six weeks of studying poetry. In that study, the class had grown accustomed to talking about the shape of poetry and how it looked on the page. As they moved into this new area of inquiry, Dan explained to them that they would go about the study of tests in the same way. "Today," he said, "look at these practice reading tests. With your partner, notice how it is set up, notice how the words go on the page in the same ways you did with poetry. Remember, don't *do* the test, *study* it. See what interesting and helpful things you can discover." José and Carmen noticed that there was a picture on some of the pages, and set out to see if looking at that picture would usually help them understand the passage. Jalyssa and Sam noted that the print was smaller and more tightly squashed together than in the books they were reading, and decided to find out if the reading of it actually was harder. Emmie and Esperanza thought the passages looked a lot longer than they could handle, and asked around for advice on how to get through them. Brian and Jason saw that the sentence at the bottom of the page always said "Go on to the next page" until there was a stop sign at the end, and that meant you were finished. They set about telling the class so no one would waste time or energy reading that sentence: this was a kind of "direction" that could be skipped, but only because the stop sign served as an additional clue.

From class to class, teachers were setting kids on the path to discovery about the layout and particulars of the genre of reading tests. Then with those discoveries as starting points, teachers and students together were inventing strategies to help them work through the tests.

Some Useful Minilessons

Directions on Reading Tests
One topic kids and teachers tackled in their inquiries was dealing with directions. For some kids "Darken each bubble very carefully" meant spending three minutes for each bubble, making sure

it was completely black and completely inside the circle. Doing this not only wastes time and energy, it makes it harder for the kids to change answers later.

Furthermore, when the directions say, "Read the entire passage and then answer the questions," some teachers and students might decide these directions should be ignored. As mentioned previously, some children might do better if they got an idea of the questions before reading the passage. However, even if the directions are to be ignored in part, *all* directions should be read carefully every time so as not to miss anything. For example, on one test we studied, students had to answer questions related to two passages and then write about those passages. Without reading the directions it would not have been clear what one was to write about. On some tests, directions give helpful tips. On the editing section of one test, the directions not only suggested categories of things to check for in editing, like punctuation, spelling, or capitalization, but also told the students how many editing mistakes to look for in the passage.

By studying old copies of their particular test, teachers can help kids figure out good ways for them to take the test. They should learn when it is important to follow the directions to the letter and when it is better to ignore part of them. Equally important is to realize that often what are called directions are actually little extras that will help students make better sense of the test: an introduction or explanation of the passage, a summary of it, or even more information about its context. One direction said something like, "This poem is about a man who lived a very *active* life," and one of the first questions following the poem was

The narrator feels that his life was

A   filled with sadness
B   too brief
C   a very busy life
D   dull and boring

Although reading the poem is the best way to get the answer, reading the orientation sentence (as a matter of course) would have helped, too.

Listening Sections of Reading Tests

When my colleagues and I first thought about the listening sections of reading tests, we could not imagine what stumbling blocks would exist relating to the format. The listening sections seemed the most straightforward—the students listen to a short story or passage and then answer some questions. Then I watched Karen Barry's third graders take a practice Educational Records Bureau (ERB) test. Karen began by passing out sheets of questions as the children found spots around the room where they would work. As soon as they were settled, Karen started to read and the children listened. It still seemed pretty straightforward to me. Then I noticed that one of the boys was staring out the window, and a little girl was slumped over the table tapping her pencil. They looked so different from the two boys sitting up front who were staring at Karen and almost nodding their heads as she read. What a difference for these two types of students when they turned to the questions! The ones who had paid sharp attention raced down the page almost as if they were afraid the story would slip from their minds. The others seemed to ramble along, sometimes skipping questions and coming back to them, making more guesses. What I had thought was straightforward no longer seemed so.

I told the children what I had noticed. I told them the important thing to do when taking the listening part of a test was to focus their minds and their bodies to avoid any distractions. We tried another listening test, this time with everyone facing the teacher, keeping their eyes focused on her, and turning their minds on "super high" to remember as much of the story as possible. This time many more students felt at ease answering the questions.

In another classroom I visited, the teacher and students were trying to figure out which was more helpful, looking at the questions as the teacher read or just listening to the story. We knew that for some tests the children did not have the questions available, but for others they did. Should they try to answer some questions as the teacher read? We discovered that more often than not, the children's attempts to answer questions during the reading made them miss parts of the story. We advised them to turn their question sheets to the blank side and just try to listen and remember the story. In these classrooms, we spent time teaching the children strategies for packing the story into their minds, as discussed in Chapter 6.

The Language of Reading Tests

Each day for a week the children in Maria Rivera's class got into partnerships and for ten minutes studied the questions on a pile of practice tests. On the morning that I visited them, Christina and Dania were in a heated discussion over the question they were studying. "What is that?" Dania asked, pointing to one of the questions. "What do they mean by pre . . . pre . . . predicate? I never heard of that before." Across the room, Ilana and Jeffrey were having a similar conversation. They were noticing that there were lots of strange words on the test that they had never heard before. They noticed words like *phrase* and *clause,* and wondered what the test makers meant by them. As Maria and I walked around the room, we suggested that the students might want to collect a list of the words that made the questions confusing for them. Then we could discuss them.

Most tests are written in a unique form of English, sometimes called super-English or hyper-English because it is exceedingly proper. For some kids, this English is not that different from their own spoken or written dialect. For other kids, however, it's very different. Therefore, it's important that teachers spend a few sessions helping all students become accustomed to the language of the tests. At the end of the class, Maria and I talked about how to help children handle unfamiliar words. As we read through the practice tests again, we realized that usually unfamiliar words that recurred on the tests came in the questions, not in the passages as we'd previously thought. The questions tended to use a certain set of words, some of which were new to the children. We knew that we needed to spend some time helping the children become familiar with the language and tone that was particular to this kind of test.

In the days after Maria's class began collecting the unfamiliar words from the test questions, we talked about these words. The children learned that more often than not, the word in the test was just another way of saying a word they already knew. To teach students this new vocabulary, Maria referred to the editing work they were doing in their writing workshop and the book talks they were having in their reading workshop. She reminded them of certain minilessons she'd taught. For example, to explain *tense agreement*, a strange phrase from the test, she explained that if you begin writing in the present, you should stay writing in the present. She went on to explain that some people call that tense agreement—staying in the same tense or time throughout a piece of writing. She offered many more examples like this, explaining how the "subject" was what they knew as the main noun in a sentence or how the "theme" was what they knew as the main message of a passage. The students then began to create lists of words, matching words they already knew to the hyper-English or Test-English equivalents. In doing this, they were relieved to realize that these strange words were actually not totally foreign to them.

Often, however, it was not just the individual words but the sound of the test as a whole that caused kids trouble. They were unaccustomed to its academic feel. One teacher suggested we might help our students become comfortable with the tone of the test by putting them in small groups to have conversations in which they tried to talk in this academic, super-English dialect, to talk the way they imagine the test makers talk while writing the tests.

How to Move Between Test Booklet and Answer Sheet

One of the most typical problems students face when taking standardized tests is dealing with the answer sheet. Often, students mark an answer to a question other than the one they are working on, or they skip a question on the test but not on the answer sheet. As we taught students to answer some questions out of order, we made it even more likely that this would occur. This problem is very damaging for students' scores because one mistake can lead to an entire sheet of incorrect answers. To avoid this, we needed to teach students some ways to ensure that their answers would be marked in the correct places on the answer sheet.

As mentioned in Chapter 6, one thing we taught students who were filling in answers out of order was to mark their answers in the test booklet before transferring them to the answer sheet. Students would therefore answer all the questions for a particular passage in the test booklet and only then would they transfer their answers to the answer sheet. That way, the students could fill in the bubbles on the answer sheet in order, leaving less room for mistakes. For other parts of the test, students developed systems for checking the bubbles. In one class, students would conduct a quick check every five questions, to match the question number to the answer number. In yet another class, every time students turned the page, they checked the answer sheet against the question they were on. In both strategies, the idea was to develop a system so that if a problem arose, students would not have to recheck every bubble, just the small section of bubbles on which they were working.

Our hope in teaching children to navigate the formats of tests was that they would come away understanding the ways in which a reading test is different from everyday reading and classwork. To do this, we studied with students the structure of the test, the various kinds of directions found within it, the requirements of the listening comprehension section, and the special hyper-language in which it's written. We also practiced the task of moving between the test booklet and the answer sheet and of filling in bubbles efficiently. This specialized technical knowledge of the test oriented us to its unique and somewhat bizarre format. Now that we knew the general lay of the land, we felt ready to face the next set of testing challenges.

8

Mastering the Tricks and Avoiding the Traps

I walked into a fifth-grade classroom recently to find the class going over the answers to a practice reading test. From the front of the room, the teacher read off the question and the answer: "Number thirteen. Something that is a 'sight for sore eyes' is (A) refreshing." Then, as an explanation, she added, "See, up in the passage it says, 'I was very thirsty. The glass of water was *a sight for sore eyes.* That's what 'a sight for sore eyes' means."

Jennifer leaned over and whispered in Sean's ear, "I can't remember all these words. I'll *never* pass this test." Many students believe that in order to do well on standardized reading tests, they need to memorize the definitions of a lot of words and to learn the answers to a lot of questions. Many teachers seem to believe this as well. Kids in classrooms across the nation do one thing, above all else, in the name of test preparation: they follow along while their teacher goes over the correct answers on practice tests they have just taken.

This is a sure-fire way for a child to make the answers on today's practice reading test match those on the answer sheet, but it's unclear whether any child learns anything that can be useful on another day on another test. The questions won't be the same on tomorrow's test. Even if Jennifer could retain the meaning of *a sight for sore eyes*, it wouldn't help her on tomorrow's test.

In their writing workshops, we advise teachers to teach the writer, not the writing. We say, "If you intervene in such a way that the writing gets better but the writer learns nothing that he can use on another day, on another piece, you've gained little. We need to teach the writer strategies that he can use on future days, in future writing."

It was only logical, then, that as we conferred with our youngsters about trying to get better at taking standardized reading tests,
and as we gathered these youngsters for whole-class demonstrations and instruction, we tried to teach the reader, not the reading.
Although we still went over the questions and talked about the
answers, our emphasis now was on the strategies children had
used or might have used to reach these answers.

We discussed with students how it's important to look for evidence from the text, instead of personal opinions, to support
answers, and how they might write key words alongside paragraphs to help them go back to the right part of the passage for
answers. Or we discussed strategies for deciding what the question is really asking. Our emphasis was always on teaching the students strategies they could use again and again, for many passages
on many tests.

Interestingly, what we were doing with test preparation exactly
paralleled what we were doing in math. At one time, students in
our math classes would have solved problems such as 168 x 23 and
our work together would have consisted of checking for correct
answers. Now our discussions in math include questions: "What
operation did you use to solve that problem? "Did anyone go
about solving the problem in a different way?" Together, we learn
a variety of ways for proceeding.

In our work with standardized tests, as in our work with
math, we began to focus less on the correct answers and more
on developing a repertoire of strategies students can use to find
answers on standardized tests. We first did this to prepare for
the type of test that consists of reading comprehension passages
followed by questions, and later to prepare for other types of
reading tests.

It wasn't immediately clear to us how we would find out which
strategies a child had used in order to answer a test question, how
we would learn the ways the child had reached her conclusions.
Should we interview the child after she had taken a practice test?
Maybe we should ask her to make notes in the margins or to
explain her thinking as she worked. Our study group tried many
different ways to get at the logic children used to complete tests;
without a doubt, the way that brought us the most information

was to watch the child as she worked on the test, interrupting her to ask questions about what we saw her doing.

At first, this way of figuring out what kids were thinking was painstaking. When we asked a child how he had gone about selecting a particular answer, the child often had little to say: "I just picked it" or "That answer just grabbed my eye." Often children would say about their chosen answer, "It stood out" or "It seemed like the best one." But we kept at it whenever we met, dividing our study group into subgroups of three, each subgroup assigned to study a child for an hour and then come back to tell the group about what had been learned.

We worked like that for awhile, scratching the dirt for the little seeds of information that the children would sometimes drop for us. Then someone in our group hit on a more effective way of working, which will always happen, it seems, if you work with a group long enough. Instead of asking a child, "Why did you choose that answer?" Jacqueline Jones asked the young boy she was interviewing, "Can you walk me through your choices? Can you tell me why you didn't choose these other answers?" When she asked the question this way, the information rained down.

Researching Your Students as Test Takers

Andrew was looking at a passage about baking a cake, one that he was clearly able to read. The first question, one he had gotten wrong, asked him which opinion from the list of answer choices was expressed in the story. "Well," Andrew began, "it can't be '(A) baking a cake isn't too hard,' because baking *is* hard. You have to measure all the ingredients just right or the cake will taste bad. When the passage said that, I thought it was a stupid idea, and not true at all. I hate it when my mom wants me to help her bake." Suddenly, with his explanation of why he didn't choose (A), the correct answer, we had a window into what Andrew was thinking. Now we knew the internal logic that had led him to the incorrect answer. Suddenly, we knew better what to teach him, how to help him get that kind of question right the next time.

In her book *Errors and Expectations* (1977), Mina Shaughnessy explains that to brush aside an error in a child's writing with a red-penned "Awkward!" or "Proofread!" is to ignore the logic that led him to the error; it's to miss the chance to see the way he thinks the rules work. The same is true for errors a child makes in any area. By looking closely at the reasoning behind the mistake, by examining the intelligence behind the error, we have an opportunity to see into a child's mind. Then, with that glimpse, our teaching can be much more effective.

If we hadn't learned Andrew's logic, we might have relied on the test makers' analysis. In many test preparation booklets and many tests, the questions are grouped into categories according to the skill a child supposedly needs to choose the right answer. If a child gets question nine wrong, for example, the test makers' analysis might say he has problems inferring; if a child misses number eleven, she has problems understanding sequence, and so on. For Andrew's mistake, the test makers concluded his problem was in recalling information. So if we had relied on this source, we would have worked on trying to boost his memory.

On our own, relying simply on knowing him and knowing his reading level, we might have concluded that he hadn't understood the passage about baking or that he had skipped the sentence about the boy saying baking would be easy. Based on this understanding, we might have advised him to reread the passage more carefully, or we might have pointed to the sentence and had him read it aloud to make sure he got it.

Now, with his thinking revealed about why he didn't choose certain options, we would teach him very differently. "Andrew," Claire said that day, having listened to his logic, "I noticed something about the way you take tests. Sometimes, you use what you know from your own life to help you understand what is in the story or in the question, don't you? That works very well for reading most books, I know, but let me tell you something. In tests, you should never count on *just* what you know from your life to give you an answer. Never. There should always be something in the passage that can give you a clue. Always. If the reason for choosing or not choosing an answer is only something you know from your life, and not from the passage, you have to think again. If you are really stuck and have no idea what the answer is from looking at the passage, then go ahead and use your experience as a resource—in that case it's a good strategy. Otherwise, it will make you get answers wrong."

Teachers will want to research their children. Although because of time constraints it will not be possible to study each child's test-taking logic and processes in depth, studying even five children will reveal worlds of thinking and may create a variety of profiles of test takers that teachers can rely on when interviewing other students. The following paragraphs describe some ideas we found helpful when researching children.

Working in research groups, even just in pairs, makes the process easier. Two or three people will have more ideas about what the child is thinking, about what will help her, and about what is getting in her way.

It's generally easier to see children's thinking at the times when they make mistakes. Because of this, it usually works best to study children as they take a test that is somewhat difficult for them. A child's individual quirky thinking is harder to see when it leads to a right answer. At the same time, if the test is much too difficult, her thinking will be equally hard to see, because she won't be able to work at a level where she can use much of it. Therefore, it is very important to find the right practice test to give a child you want to study.

When studying children, watching carefully will provide just as much information as listening carefully. Watch where their eyes move, when they seem to get restless or troubled, when their concentration seems to be kicking in, when they use their pencil, when they use their finger, and so on. All these behaviors can be the basis for questions: When you started biting your pencil, what were you thinking? When you began to point, how was that helping? Another reason to watch is that, in many cases, what children say they do or think they do is not at all the same as what they actually do when they sit down to take a test. If our study group had a nickel for every child who claimed to read the questions first when taking a test but who, when observed, read the passage without even a glance at the questions, we would all be rich.

As much as possible, have students *do* something based on what you have noticed about them as test takers. For example, if you see a child who seems to be reading well but doesn't seem to be answering the questions well, you might ask him to say the questions in his own words, as I describe later in this chapter. By having the child act on your hunches, by asking him to do something specifically in the area on which you want to focus your attention, you can deepen your investigation. If he has no problem asking the question in his own words, maybe his problem wasn't misunderstanding the question, and you have to keep on researching. On the other hand, if he does have trouble, you can begin to look at what part of it is difficult for him, and why.

Here are questions that helped us as we interviewed kids:

- Why did/didn't you choose *this* answer? And why/why not *this* one? And *this* one?
- What was your thinking as you worked through this question? Can you show me all the thinking you went through before you came to this answer?
- I noticed you doing . . . . Why? Why did you look up at the first paragraph/look down at the question/turn back the page/stop for a minute/do it quickly/do it slowly/roll your eyes?
- Interrupt them to ask, What are you doing/thinking/where are you looking right now?
- When you have a hunch or theory, ask a particular question to confirm or disprove it: Do you know what that word means? Is all the print on this page distracting you, or is it fine? Do you think this is a confusing question?

Don't accept the first (usually empty) answer. Very often, when I asked students to explain their answers, they responded by reading parts of the passage. They found it difficult to explain what they were thinking or doing. I might assist them by saying, "I have a couple of guesses about what you might be trying to do/what you might be thinking right now. Are any of these similar to what you *really* are trying/thinking?" Over time, because students will internalize your expectation that they have chosen their answers for a reason, they will become more articulate at explaining those reasons. They will come to anticipate your questions and will already be thinking of their answers.

Overall, the most important piece of advice on how to research kids well is to always have the attitude that the child chose the answer he did, that the child is working the way he is working, for a reason; it might be a wrong reason, but it exists. He has a rationale for his behavior, and if you can discover this rationale, and if you can teach into it and away from it, that will be the key to improving the child's ability to work well.

Some Strategies to Teach

Use the Text, Not Your Life, to Pick Your Answer

Many children we studied fell into the same trap that Andrew fell into. When it came to choosing an answer, they were much more likely to turn to their own memories or experiences than to turn to the hard-to-understand text for their answers. For a passage about cowboys, Frank told us he had chosen an answer for one question because it was like that in the cowboy movies he watched on TV Saturday afternoons. And for a passage on hamburgers, Jennifer told us she had picked an answer because it was "true." "I picked '(B) Americans like hamburgers' because it's true. Whenever I go to a restaurant with my friends, everyone wants a hamburger. It's what we all like best." This issue became even more difficult when the passage was an excerpt from a text with which the students were familiar. Many new reading tests use passages from some of our children's favorite literature, including those stories that have been made into movies. We might see tests with excerpts from *Charlotte's Web* or *Charlie and the Chocolate Factory*. In this case, students were justifying their answers by referring to the movies or their memory of hearing the story when they were younger.

While these personal connections are helpful if the student is at a complete loss for an answer, it's essential that children understand that relying on opinions, memories, or personal experience is not a reliable strategy for finding answers that a test maker has decided are correct. Clearly, many questions asked on the tests require prior knowledge to answer: knowing about the desert helps answer questions about Egypt. But the problem comes when students rely exclusively on that prior knowledge, ignoring the information presented in the passage. We therefore began teaching minilessons that would support the kids' abilities to find answers that are generally agreed to and that could be supported by evidence from the passage.

In Chapter 6, I discussed the minilessons my colleagues and I taught to help kids read the passages. One strategy was to underline parts of the passage that might be asked about in the questions. In teaching the children to find evidence for their answers in the passages instead of in their lives, we first had them return to the underlined parts of the passage. Then if the underlined parts didn't support their answer, they were to look elsewhere in the passage for evidence. For cloze-style tests, we taught the children to ask themselves what the paragraph was mainly about, instead of turning to their own life experiences to choose an answer. All the answer choices in many of the tests make grammatical sense in the sentence, and so we needed to teach kids strategies that would help them choose the word that matched the meaning of the passage instead of the individual sentence or their own experiences.

Sometimes It's Important to Refer to Your Life

While it is essential for the reading comprehension sections of a reading test that kids find evidence in the passages to support their answers, there are parts of many tests where the only things students can rely on are their own previous experiences. In these separate sections, students are often asked to choose the correct spelling of the underlined word from among four choices or to choose the word whose meaning is closest to that of the underlined word. There is no context within the test from which to choose an answer, so students have to rely on their outside knowledge.

Often, students prepared for these sections of the tests by taking practice tests and then going over the answers in the same way as was described at the beginning of this chapter. But, again, would these words ever appear on the actual test? We knew we needed to teach strategies that would help the students no matter what words were on the test. We decided to begin by researching students who scored very high on these sections to see what strategies they used for selecting their answers.

I began by watching Naydine work on the vocabulary section of a practice CTBS. I decided to watch her because her teacher told me that she not only scored very well on this part of the test but that she was, in fact, one of the strongest readers in the class. Along with always being in the midst of reading a novel, Naydine often created small reading projects for herself. For example, she might gather up a pile of Langston Hughes poems, practice reading them aloud, and then give a poetry reading for her family. In conversations about books, Naydine asked big questions about books and often compared different books the class was reading. I was particularly interested as to whether and how this thoughtfulness would translate to the test. Naydine began by reading the directions and understood that she had to choose the word that meant the same thing as the underlined word. Then she turned her attention to the first question, "*snoozing* lightly." She quickly bubbled in "(C) napping," explaining to me that in the books she's read "whenever there's the word *snoozing*, someone's napping." The next word to be defined was "*sparkle* brightly." In choosing her answer, "(B) twinkle," Naydine explained that she didn't remember seeing *sparkle* in any books she's read, but she knew it had to do with light because of the word *brightly*, so she chose "twinkle." Again, Naydine had referred to her own reading to choose her answer. She continued work on this section the same way.

I decided to explore her process little more. "Naydine," I started, "I notice that for each of these questions you chose your answer based on your own reading; can you tell me about that?"

"It's like, for each one I first say 'have I ever seen that in a book before?' and if I have, I try to think about what it meant in the book. Then I choose. But sometimes it doesn't work. So I have to think about where else I might have heard that word before."

I was astounded at how Naydine explicitly used her reading to answer the questions. It was one thing to know the research that showed that students' vocabulary was best improved by reading, that the students who scored well on the SAT tests were also the students who read a lot, but here was a student who was referring to her own reading as an explicit strategy for taking a vocabulary test. Her way was different from the strategies that I had been teaching students previously. I had told my students to think of the definition of the underlined word and then choose the word that means almost the same thing. Here, Naydine was creating a context for the words. I knew I would have to teach the rest of the class to ask the questions Naydine was asking: "Have I seen this word before in a book?" "Where have I heard that before?" "What words or events usually happen around it?"

This idea of recreating a context for the word seemed helpful for the spelling sections of the tests as well. I watched Robert try it. For each word, he would close his eyes, imagine himself spelling the word, and then check to see if his spelling was among the choices. For Robert, who was a powerful speller, this was a sound strategy. Other students, whose spelling was not as strong, would close their eyes and try to picture the word in a book they had read and check that image against the answer choices.

Learn to Read the Questions

We had always assumed that if the kids had reading troubles, it would be with reading the difficult passages. As it turned out, the passages usually weren't the hardest part for the students. Despite the fact that the test was filled with excerpts from other texts and that some of them were poorly written, the kids still had reading experiences to draw upon to read them. In the end, reading the questions, a much less familiar task, often proved to be the greatest reading challenge for them.

The questions were alien: "How was the central problem resolved?" "What unexpected event happened while the boys were in the basement?" "Which statement is NOT true about the narrator?" "What conclusion can you draw from this passage?" These were not the types of questions children were asking themselves and each other about the books they were reading. In our reading workshops, children were asking questions such as "What was your favorite part?" "Would you have done what the mother did at the end of the story?" "How is the brother in this book like the brother in the last book we read?" "What was the story *really* about?"

Many teachers began to spend time studying question types with their students. Together they searched through the practice tests and made lists of the types of questions that were asked. They studied the different ways the test asked the same question. For example, the kids began to understand that "What's the best title for this story?" and "This story is mostly about . . ." were both questions asking for the main idea of the passage.

They paid particular attention to questions that were asked over and over again. My colleagues and I studied a variety of test practice books, looking most closely at the one that was used by our teachers around the city. We looked at the kinds of questions that were emphasized. We noticed that the practice test often had a question with "NOT," for example, "Which of the following is NOT true?" Also, it often had questions asking for definitions of words. Every passage was followed by at least one of each of these questions. Every passage was also followed by a question asking about the main idea: "A good title for this selection is . . ." or "The central problem of this story is . . . " Several teachers spent a few hours helping their students understand what these three kinds of questions meant and making sure that they learned how to answer them.

When the actual test came, these teachers scanned it as the kids were working. They found that there were tremendous differences between the questions from the test practice book and those that were on the actual test. They told us that there was only one "NOT" question on the test but many asking the students to think about why something probably happened or what something probably meant. Furthermore, on the actual test, the questions asking for the passage's main message were worded in yet different ways from those on the practice test, for example, "What does the author probably want you to learn from the story?"

The city had spent hundreds of thousands of dollars on test preparation materials—materials that appeared to the official ones—and yet we discovered many differences between those materials and the actual test. Who was checking to see whether these materials in fact represented the format and content of the real tests? We learned that in working with kids on reading test questions, we have to be very careful to teach not only the particulars but also more general insights.

Besides working with kids on understanding different types of questions, we worked with them on learning to read a whole series of questions, expecting each to require a different kind of work. On tests like the Terra Nova, where questions about sentence combining, vocabulary, and general literary knowledge all follow the reading passages, students were constantly having to change the work they were doing, and this confused them. For example, "What is the passage mostly about?" might be followed by a time line of the passage to be filled in by the student. The next question might ask students to edit a paragraph related to the story, and next they might have to do sentence combining. After taking this test many students described a feeling of confusion about which stories to keep in mind or a feeling of being jerked here and there. And they were. Because of this, we knew that students needed to treat reading the questions with the same seriousness and the same strategies as they did for reading the passages. We taught some kids to read the questions like Julian, who kept rereading with an emphasis on important words until he was able to say, "O.K., I got it." Others we taught to work like Stuart, who underlined key words in the editing question in order to remember how many and what kind of mistakes to search for.

Choose the Answer to the Question

As Sam was taking a practice reading test, I noticed that he kept looking between the passage and the question as he worked his way down the page. He appeared to be moving along confidently. But when I looked over his answers, I could see that most of them were wrong. I watched him while he worked on question number eleven:

The central problem of the tale is that

> A   Doug and Al are pals and like to go on treasure hunts.
> B   Don loves to build things.
> C   The alarm clock rang.
> D   Doug, Al, and Don got locked in the attic.

Sam chose (A), a wrong answer again, so I asked him to explain his thinking. "I didn't have to read past (A)," Sam says, "I knew it was the right answer right away because, look! Here the first sentence of the passage says "Doug and Al were pals, they liked to go on treasure hunts." He had missed that the question asked for "the central problem."

I could see that Sam often chose his answers in this way, by finding the first answer choice that matched something in the text. Over and over again, he explained why he had selected an answer by pointing to an identical phrase in the passage, as if the fact that these words were actually in the passage proved he was right. Unfortunately for Sam, the answers he was choosing weren't related to the questions. If the test asked him "Which event happened last in the story?" he was apt to choose the first answer he read that matched an event in the story, not considering whether it was the last event, as the question demanded.

Sam was falling into a typical trap set by test makers. He was not considering what the question was asking but instead was being seduced by facts of the story that were repeated in the answer choices.

Because so many students in the class had fallen into this trap along with Sam, we decided to spend some time helping kids turn their attention to the questions. The next day, we called the children together and gave them yet another passage from another practice test. This time, we told the children to focus their attention on the questions, and to try to think about exactly what was being asked. I explained to them, "Often when I take a test like this, after reading the question, I stop and try to figure out what information the question wants me to get. I'll show you. Let's look at the first one. 'What is Ralph's main concern?' I stop and say to myself, 'Okay, they want me to find out what this guy Ralph is mostly worried about.' Can you see how I tried to figure out what they were asking by trying to say the question in my own words? Let's begin our work today by trying this strategy with a partner. Read the question, figure out with your partner what it's asking, and write down what you decide. When you are finished, put your paper in this basket and go off to work on your own test practice."

After watching and conferring with the children that day, after seeing their written work and their struggles in trying to understand the questions, we knew we needed to continue working on this topic. To do this, I compiled a list of some of the ways the children had rephrased each question:

Test Question	The Ways Students Paraphrase the Question
Why did Ralph want to stay?	Why does the guy want to stay? We need to find out why Ralph wants to stay together with his friend. Where does Ralph want to stay? Why didn't Ralph want to go home?
When did Ralph return?	What time did Ralph return? Why did Ralph come again? When did he come back? How are you going to come back?
Why did Ralph lose the dog Blacktail?	I have to find out why did Ralph's dog lost the Blacktail. I have to find why Ralph lost the dog. Why did Ralph lose his black tail? Why was the dog Blacktail important?

Together, we looked at the questions and their paraphrased counterparts. The kids were surprised when they realized how different some interpretations of the questions were from the questions themselves. With partners, they discussed which interpretations would help them and which would lead them astray. Over the next few days' doing this together as a class, in partners, and individually, the kids became much more adept at understanding what a question required them to do. No longer, we hoped, would they be seduced by an answer that matched the text if that wasn't what the question called for.

Years ago, Flower and Hayes (1980) wrote an article about the different ways children answer essay questions. They had found that students who tended to write fuller, more thoughtful essays were answering a different question than those who had written more sparse answers. In one case, children had clearly thought about the question and what it could mean and did mean to them. In the other, the children had often latched onto just one word in the question and written about things in their minds triggered by that word. They recommended in that study that children should take a moment before answering a question to really hold that question in their minds, look it over, roll it around, and mull it over. This seemed to help children work with essay questions more successfully. Their work seemed to loosely parallel our work in this case. Our minilessons about paraphrasing the question, holding onto the question for a moment, seemed to help children focus on what the test makers wanted and seemed to help them get more right answers. Of course, since standardized multiple-choice tests aren't calling for deep, thoughtful, creative answers, there is a balance to be maintained between understanding the question's intent, and overthinking it.

Risk an Unfamiliar Choice

Kendra began to read the first passage on the practice cloze-type test by leaning her face on her arms and reading in a whispery voice. She read the entire paragraph and then turned her attention to the answer choices.

> All plants get food from the earth. Some plants also need meat. These plants are _____. One of these strange plants is called the Venus flytrap.

>   A   fat
>   B   round
>   C   dry
>   D   blue
>   E   unusual

"It can't be dry," Kendra said, "because it didn't say anything about no water." She picked up her pencil and crossed out answer choice (C). "It can't be fat or round because plants aren't ever fat and round. And it doesn't say anything about blue either." Kendra crossed out answer choices (A), (B), and (D), and looked over the paragraph again. "Well, I guess it's (B)," she said, and bubbled in that answer. At this point, I asked her what she was thinking about answer (E). Kendra told me she didn't know that word, so she couldn't choose it. She was more willing to choose an unlikely answer, one she had already ruled out, than to choose a word she didn't know.

This was the fourth time in this class I had seen a child avoid an unknown word even when the other choices were probably wrong, so I put the passage onto an overhead for the next day's lesson. I gathered the children, and using the overhead, Kendra explained her thinking of the day before. She told the children how she hadn't chosen the word she didn't know, choosing one that was probably wrong instead. She went on to explain how in my conference with her I had encouraged her to choose that strange word when the other choices had been eliminated. She and I advised the others to try that, and they went off to work. During our sharing time that day, the children who had chosen unknown words as answers shared their experiences, and the lesson seemed to have helped them.

Use Elimination to Choose One Answer

Teachers often try to teach children a way to narrow down the answer choices through the process of elimination. Across the country, we hear that, for any given test question, one answer choice will be silly—way out of the range of possible, with scarcely any connection to the answer, and one answer choice will probably be the opposite of the right answer. Of the two remaining possibilities, one will be very close to the right answer, and one will *be* the right answer. It will usually be hard to tell which of the last two is correct.

Many students eliminate two possibilities and then, from the last two, just sort of pick one. They don't, it seems, try to figure out a reason to choose one over the other. They seem to wrongly assume that the two choices left are equally possible. Andreas had to answer this question from a practice test: "How was the problem resolved?" Andreas knew that two of the choices were incorrect, but he was unsure of the other two. He explained that it could be either choice, it didn't matter which one he chose: (F) was a good answer, or it could be (G). Often in our research we saw that students like Andreas would, at this point in their thinking, randomly select between answers (F) and (G), believing that both were correct. We took steps to clarify our teaching of the process of elimination to be sure that Andreas knew there was only one correct answer, and he was to choose it from the two remaining possibilities.

Check Your Answers

As Maria reached the last question on the last page of her practice reading test, I noticed a small smile cross her lips. I could almost see inside her head. "Whew," she must have been thinking. "I'm done." I leaned over to her and whispered in her ear, "Have you checked your answers?" The smile disappeared as Maria opened her practice booklet to the first passage. I think so many students feel the same sense of dread when asked that question.

In our research, we tried to figure out what it was that made checking the answers so dreadful. We watched our test takers and asked them about this, only to discover that the biggest reason kids hated checking answers was because they had only one strategy for doing so. Most students were like Maria: they opened their test booklets to the first passage and began again. To them, checking answers meant taking the test again. No wonder so many students never check their answers. No wonder others take an extraordinary amount of time to finish their tests. No wonder they are then so exhausted and overwhelmed.

We knew we needed to teach strategies for selectively going back through the test and reconsidering answers. Kathleen Tolan began this work in her classroom by referring to a math problem the class had been working on earlier in the day. "This morning as we worked on our division problems, we discovered that when we check our math, we don't do it by solving every problem on the page over again using the same strategies we used to solve them initially. We realized we could check only the problems we were unsure of, and we did so by solving the problem in a different way." Kathleen went on to explain to the class that the same idea was important in testing. "If we check our answers by taking the entire test again in the same way, we might not catch mistakes that we've made. We need some new strategies for checking answers."

Over the next few days Kathleen and many other teachers began teaching strategies for checking answers. The first issue to address was which questions to revisit. We discussed how it was unnecessary to return to answers about which they felt fairly confident. Instead, we taught them to develop a system to keep track of the questions that gave them trouble. Some kids kept a small scrap of paper next to them and jotted down the numbers of the questions they wanted to return to. Others circled the number in their test booklet or answer sheet. Still others knew that particular types of questions gave them trouble and so those were the ones that called for checking. For some kids the trouble questions were "NOT" questions: "Which statement is NOT true according to the story?" Other children struggled over questions asking for a main idea.

Still others knew they just didn't have the energy to go over their answers at the end of the test and would instead check confusing questions after each passage as they finished it. For every child we suggested taking a short bathroom or drink break before checking answers to give the child's mind a chance to clear a bit. In every case, children devised a personalized way of keeping track of which questions they needed to double-check and which they didn't.

When we first set out to help children master the tricks and avoid the traps of reading tests, we knew that telling them the right answers on one particular test probably wouldn't help them on the next test. We knew that we needed to teach them ways to find correct answers again and again, on test after test. To do this, we studied the ways our kids were already working. Earlier in this chapter, we offered some advice for teachers who want to do this. We knew that we had to look at the unhelpful patterns of thinking and the misguided processes of test taking that were leading our kids to the wrong answers. Once we had uncovered a bunch of these common mistakes, we were able to point them out to the children and teach them how to change their habits. Kids who had previously turned to their life experiences to answer questions began to turn to the passages first. Students who had skimmed over the test questions now paused, concentrating on them for a moment. The children began justifying their answers, even when using the process of elimination. Again and again, we saw evidence that kids can improve and change their test-taking habits if we teach them about their misleading work patterns. Teaching children about the traps they tend to fall into may well be the most powerful, specific preparation we can give them for the day of the test.

9

The Terrible, Horrible,
No Good, Very Bad Day

Test Day. It's a bad day for the kids, but at least *I* know *my* role. For me as a teacher, testing day had never been too bad because at least as a proctor I knew what to do. The test preparation phase always felt complicated—I was damned if I did it (I worried that my progressive ancestors would turn in their graves) and damned if I didn't. But when it came to proctoring for the test, I had my script in hand. With great firmness and resolution, I'd rearrange the desks, separating each into an island. I knew absolutely, unambivalently that my students needed to bring three No. 2 pencils to school on Test Day. I put that in the letter home, along with the part about getting a good night's sleep and a healthy breakfast. Absolutely and unambivalently I assigned the seats, and absolutely and unambivalently I delivered the Test-Taking Address. "Today, you will respect each other's personal space," I announced. "Our eyes will not wander. Hands on the desk, eyes on the page. There will be no talking and no touching."

It was only fair. A standardized test means standard conditions, and if I believe that all children should get equal treatment, then I had to put my heart into making conditions as standard as they could be. And then I heard about the school where, in order to be fair, in order to eliminate differences in the way teachers read aloud, students all took the test in the cafeteria and heard the test directions booming down at them through the school's public address system. Such impersonal and intimidating formality in the name of standardization distressed me. Did it have to be this way?

Then, in our study group, conversations opened about proctoring and about setting up standardized conditions for taking the tests. As we began talking, this topic, which had once seemed so unambiguous, so set and clear, suddenly began to seem complicated, confusing, and newly full of possibilities.

As we started describing the standard conditions each of us had put in place for the day of the test, we saw that, despite our best intentions to follow the rules so that our testing sites would all be the same, in most cases we had been creating completely different "standard" conditions.

One teacher thought it was standard practice to write the time on the board and change it every fifteen minutes, while others assumed that no one was allowed to write anything on the board at all during the test. While some teachers thought the kids had to be separated by cardboard dividers to prevent cheating, others thought they need only set kids up two per table instead of four. We differed about everything from what was allowed to be on the classroom walls, to whether we were allowed to tell a student if we noticed him filling in bubble number five for question number four, to what kinds of questions we were allowed to answer during the test. We were shocked to realize how unstandard the standardized conditions for our test were. The one part of testing that had once seemed so clear now felt confusing.

Once the conversation opened, many of us admitted to feeling awkward and afraid on testing day. We didn't really know what was legal and what was illegal. "Truthfully, I never know if I'm supposed to walk around during the test or just sit in a chair and watch the kids," one person said. "Sometimes I feel like I just want to rub a student's shoulders. Do other people do that?" another asked. "I never know what I can say and what I can't. Am I going to be caught, convicted, dragged out of there in handcuffs? My heart beats wildly if I tell a child 'Slow down, you're rushing!' Whatever I do on testing day, I feel like I'm driving with a police car behind me—even if I'm totally legal, I clench the wheel and keep my eye on the rearview mirror, sure that at any moment the flashing light and siren will start."

All these differences could be corrected, all these anxieties calmed, we thought, if we could read for ourselves ahead of time the instruction booklet that usually comes in the package with the sets of tests. If we could only get our hands on them sooner, so that we could plan! So we set off on a quest to find the booklets, to principals' offices, district offices, and old file cabinets, through test publishing companies, experts, and researchers. And with some effort, we got our hands on the instruction booklets. Some of them.

What does that mean about standard conditions, we thought, if teachers rarely have the booklets that define the conditions for the tests until the day of the test—too late, in most cases, to interpret and carry out its instructions for setting up and for proctoring? How standard can they then be? In addition, we found that many of the booklets we had finally managed to acquire were in fact written and distributed not by the testing companies, as we had thought, but instead by people working in district offices. This meant that although the text of the test might be the same for everyone, the accepted rules about the conditions for taking it could, and probably would, vary from school to school or district to district.

And what if all those booklets *were* the same, and all schools *did* have them on hand before the tests, and all teachers *did* conscientiously try to follow the regulations set out in their pages, would the conditions for the tests be standard then? In some ways, we agreed, they might be close. But in other ways, even in an extreme and improbable situation like that, inequalities would still exist. In some classrooms, the nearby subway train would rattle students every few minutes, leaving behind a trail of smelly exhaust. In others, children would work in peaceful silence, disturbed only by an occasional songbird. In some classrooms, the students would be hungry and tired, frightened by the strange and intimidating formality of testing day. In others, the kids would greet the test with rosy-cheeked health, unfazed by the changes this day brings.

Many principled educators have decided that, despite the obstacles, they will try their best to standardize conditions on testing day. Knowing that limitations will always exist, they will still make their best effort to keep all schools in their district or all teachers in their school on a script within certain confines for the day of the test. These educators believe that their primary responsibility to children is to standardize test-taking conditions even beyond what the booklets prescribe.

At the same time, there are principled educators who have made a different choice about how to handle standardization. These educators also carefully follow the regulations for establishing testing conditions. The difference between them and their colleagues is their belief that after the rules have been satisfied, their primary responsibility is to provide their students with the conditions that will most support their reading abilities, the conditions that will optimize their scores. By putting their kids in the best allowable situation, the kids' scores will reflect their classroom reading abilities more closely. Increasing the correlation between what the students can do and what the scores report they can do is more important to these educators than increasing the standardization. In fact, the American Psychological Association (APA) guidelines for testing advocate that conditions under which children take standardized tests should mirror as closely as possible their natural learning environment. We talked to many of these educators about exactly what they did on testing day, within the regulations of their own particular tests.

Setting up the Room for Test Day

For me, the first surprise was that for many tests, there was some flexibility in the allowable arrangement of furniture. I'd always assumed that children were required to sit at separate desks. This meant that when I was a teacher the entire tone of my classroom changed on test day; it was as if a different order reigned. Beneath the regimentation, one could see remnants of a cozy, child-centered classroom, but on test day, rows of desks covered the library carpet, and our Author's Chair was sent into the corner to stand with its face to the wall.

Other educators had made similar assumptions about what was necessary. Some had moved their children to the cafeteria or to the lecture hall so they could seat one child per table. One teacher, who'd taught all year with her children sitting at tables and on carpets, had packed her entire room with forty-two desks that day. Another had made elaborate cardboard "cubbies," which she set up around each child's patch of table space.

But other teachers, who were also following the testing regulations very carefully, were appalled to think of the stomach cramps and clenched jaws we would create by totally altering the landscape of our classrooms to try to create standard conditions on testing day. In Kathy Doyle's fifth-grade class, she and the students had together explored ways to arrange their classroom to create the conditions every child would need on the day of the test in order to focus intensely. Some children moved their desks against a wall, some chose a portion of a table or even a corner of the carpet as their work space. Then, before testing day, each child tried out his or her space, and the class as a whole grew comfortable with the revised layout of the room.

In his classroom, Dan Harper simply brought in an additional table or two so the kids could sit three rather than four per table. He also made special arrangements for two of his children to take their tests in the reading resource room. "For these kids, the resource room is where they feel safest and most supported," he explained. "They need the smaller space and Claire's comforting presence. I also wanted them to be away from the whiz kids who might finish the test early and add to their tension."

As we asked, we found that teachers also had very different ways of dealing with the materials on their walls. I had always thought that it was illegal to have anything—charts, lists, diagrams—on the walls of my classroom during testing time. I figured any material with writing on it was against the rules. So on the morning before the test I would strip the walls bare and staple construction paper over any writing I couldn't take down. I scoured the room to find any chart of reading skills that might somehow have an answer on it. I knew the room looked shockingly stark on the morning of the test, but this seemed only proper. In some states, including Texas, this is necessary, but in others, the regulations don't call for this. "The only restriction for us is that you can't put up new stuff the day before or the day of the test," teachers from another state explained. "We always make sure to hang *bunches* of charts about test-taking strategies— but at least a week before the test, so it's fair and square!" After reading countless instruction manuals, we learned that bare walls are not always the rule, so if teachers are interested in both following the rules and maximizing the help they can give their students within these rules, they will have to read the instruction booklets for themselves.

Setting a Tone for Test Day

Every teacher has stories of children dissolving into tears, vomiting, or peeing in their pants on the day of the tests, and even if their feelings aren't so obvious, we know that all our children feel the pressure.

Many people we spoke to regarded easing students' tension as a top priority, and most teachers had invented ways to at least poke a hole in the problem. One let students chew gum on that day, another played Bach in the early morning hours, and another brought a surprise snack for them to munch on.

What impressed me the most, however, was that some teachers felt that the pressure didn't emanate from the test booklets. They had realized that often we ourselves create the very stress that we then try to relieve. "I think I'm really the source of the most tension," said one teacher. "As test day draws nearer, I know my nerves get frayed. I snap at the kids more quickly, I act high strung." Others agreed. "I pick up the tension my principal feels," one said. "We all do. The whole school becomes a tightly wound spring ready to snap." These teachers explained to us that in order to really defuse the tension, they needed to go beyond simply making small changes to the daily routine to focus on the entire context of the test, which includes the teacher.

"I tell myself that the kids deserve better," one teacher said. "I make a point to have our days be as serene and as loving as possible. Especially on the day of the test, I refrain from jumping on a kid for some small misbehavior. 'Let it go,' I say to myself, and if they forget their pencils that day, or get to school late, I go overboard to smooth things out. This isn't the day to focus on holding kids accountable for coming to school prepared."

Kathy Doyle told us that she sets a supportive tone for that day by arranging for a communal breakfast. A few parents help, and together they serve the children muffins, fruit juice, and yogurt in class. "This way, we as a class have some nice time together to chat about the upcoming test," she explained, "and I know they've had a healthy breakfast."

In Mark Hardy's classroom, testing day begins just as writing celebrations do. The students gather on the rug, and Mark talks about the skills he's seen them developing for dealing with tests, and he tells them that the test is a celebration of all they have learned this year about test preparation. Before the children disperse to their "testing nooks," they recall in their response groups the pieces of advice they're going to follow for the day. Mark circulates among the groups, adding some quiet, final words. "Evan, remember to slow down, this isn't a race. Charleen, I have the feeling this is going to be your day, I can feel it in my bones, the test will look hard at first, but it's not going to faze you!"

Kristen Eagleburger set particular goals for the tone of her class. "My kids would get depressed and resigned in anticipation of the tests," she explained. "We had to do something to break the mood." To help the kids get excited, to help them take an active stance, Kristen had all the kids make paper hats for themselves to wear during the test. They decorated them with motivational sayings, "Just do it" or "Hot thinker." "It was just fun," she said, "and now they were looking forward to test day when they could wear the hats!" The students also established a ritual for that day. Just before the practice tests or actual tests began, they would huddle together, put one hand each in the center of the huddle, and then all together like a sports team, they would punch their hands into the air letting out various victory yelps. "It got them really psyched up," Kristen explained, "and it helped them remember they weren't in this alone."

In some schools in San Antonio, the whole school pitches in on testing day. Teachers from the primary grades, old friends of the kids, join the upper-grade teachers proctoring in order to create an even warmer, more supportive context for the children during the exams.

A few teachers took the idea of creating a larger supportive context for the kids even one step further. As they put it, teachers aren't the only ones to set the tone for test-taking day; parents are part of this effort as well. While Kristen leads a cheer, while Mark quietly fills a child's ear with words of support, that child's parent may well be filling the other ear with disparaging remarks. "You're never going to amount to anything if you don't do better on this year's test," a parent might be saying. "If you don't score high, your friends will be playing all summer and you'll be sitting and suffering in hot summer school." We were excited to realize that just as teachers need to coach parents in helpful ways to support their sons and daughters as they read and write, teachers also need to coach parents in helpful ways to support their child's needs as a test taker.

We pulled out letters we had written home and began to look more closely at them. Diane read aloud a letter that began like this:

> Dear Parents,
>
> I am writing to notify you that next Monday your child will take the Degrees of Reading Power examination. The scores from this test become a part of your child's permanent record. It is vital, therefore, that you ensure that your child receives a good night's sleep on the night prior to the test, and eats a full, healthy breakfast. . . .

At this point in the letter we interrupted her. A letter like this could do some good, we were thinking, making it more likely the child would have a good breakfast in the morning. But it could also do a lot of damage by fanning the fires of parental anxiety about the test, and by making it all the more likely that parents would imbue the scores with tremendous authority. Maybe the easier way to make sure kids have a good breakfast is to provide them with one on that day. Diane read more:

> . . . Please impress upon your child the importance of these tests, and do all that you can to ensure he or she achieves the highest possible standard. The scores will be sent to you immediately upon our receipt of them.
> Sincerely,
> Your Child's Teacher

Looking over the letter, we thought that perhaps it should be phrased in a totally different way. Instead of emphasizing the importance of tests, it should dissipate parental anxiety and help parents realize that, for the most part, the scores are minimally important compared with the other information the school and the teachers have about any one child's reading abilities. With this study group discussion in mind, I worked with a private school to write this letter:

> Dear Parents,
> We are writing to remind you that every year we spend a few days in the middle of October giving our students a stan-

dardized test, the Educational Records Bureau (ERB). We give this test primarily because it helps us to see trends and patterns across all our students, and helps us to see strengths and weaknesses in our instructional program. It's rare, however, that the tests provide us with new information about individual students. We, like you, already know your child well and have countless kinds of evidence of his or her skill levels. If a child's scores on the reading portion of this test are surprising, it's often because the child found the format of the standardized test strange, or because the child had a bad day. So we are writing to tell you that the tests will be taking place and to encourage you not to pay undue attention to them.

Although we don't see the test as a very important indicator of your child's strengths as a student or as a reader, we do feel that one of our responsibilities over the next ten years will be to help children handle standardized tests as well as possible. Gradually, we'll begin teaching your child strategies to work through difficulties that are not in reading but are in test taking, and those problems should dissipate over the next ten years.

It's important that students approach the test with seriousness and confidence. We encourage you to join us in cheering your child on, and in dispelling any small anxieties he or she may have.

If you want to see your child's scores, feel free to ask Ms. Rivera in the Main Office after March 30.
Sincerely,
Director of the Lower School

Proctoring

We had gathered a lot of information about writing helpful letters to parents, about setting up the room, about creating a supportive context for children on testing day. But I think the most important discussions we had were about how teachers worked during the actual test. We found that every teacher has to decide what kind of work she will do in four areas of proctoring: beginning the test, pacing, helping kids use strategies, and if permissible, gathering notes for later use.

Beginning the Test

When my colleagues suggested we needed to discuss the various ways we introduced the test and the testing session, I felt stumped. "You don't *do* anything—you simply lead them through the sample question and tell them to turn the page and begin," I thought. Talking with other teachers changed my mind. These are some of the things some teachers reminded kids about just before the test began:

- to use the strategies they know work for them, such as looking briefly through the whole test or a whole section, or reading some of the questions to get the lay of the land
- to check to see how many pages the test or section has in order to get an idea for pacing
- to star some passages that at a glance look interesting or easy (perhaps short passages for one child or poetry for another) in order to give them something to look forward to, to give them a more positive attitude
- to mark on the test booklet the places where they would plan to take short breathers to clear their heads between passages or simply to gather up their concentration for a moment
- to write "CB!" for "Check Bubbles!" at the bottom of each page, so that they would remember to make sure they had been filling in the bubble numbers that matched the question numbers (suggested by Kathleen Tolan)
- to guess when they have no idea or to leave the bubbles blank when they have no idea (depending on whether that particular test is scored by counting right answers or by deducting wrong ones)
- to note the answers they want to go back and check by recording question numbers on a piece of scrap paper or circling the numbers in the test booklet
- to rely on the strategies they've been using during all their test preparation sessions—reading the questions before the passages, underlining key words or phrases, going slowly, eliminating answers, and so on

Pacing

Within the boundaries of regulations for the tests, teachers also invented ways of helping students pace themselves. This was true regardless of whether a test was timed because, after all, most kids have limited stamina, and after they have been working on a test for an hour or so, it's almost as if their time *is* up. Teachers had the following to say about pacing:

- I remind kids before the test of all they've worked on about pacing. I know that under pressure kids tend to go back to their old ways of working, either moving too slowly and carefully to get to enough questions, or buzzing through far too fast to get them all right. I ask them to keep trying to work at the speed they know to be best for them.
- I announce the time (or write it on the chalkboard) every fifteen minutes, along with the number of the question they should probably be working on or nearly working on in order to finish before the deadline or before their stamina finishes.
- If I see a child spending an extra long time on a question during the test, I quietly remind him to guess, or to write down the number of the question to go back to at the end, and to go on to the next one.
- If I see a child speeding through the test, I check to see if they are filling in the bubbles randomly. I look to see if the bubbles are filled in to make a cute design. If it's very early in the test, I might remind the child to slow down and consider the questions more carefully. If it's late in the test, and I know that my district is able to invalidate a test that is clearly randomly answered, I might let the child continue and then invalidate the test later. Teachers will probably want to check to see if this matches their district's policy.
- As I walk around, I note which number each particular child is working on. When I pass by later, I compare the lapsed time to the number of questions the child has finished. Then, if necessary, I would advise the child to speed up or slow down depending on that child's needs.

Helping Kids Use Strategies

When we talked to teachers about what they did during the actual test itself, in that time between when children open the test booklets and when they close them and put down their pencils, there were a variety of answers because of the different regulations in different states and for different tests.

Some teachers, because of their particular school and their particular test, were constrained to say not a word during the test. "I keep quiet and shake my head at them when they raise their hands. They know I can't answer questions on this day." One teacher, on the other hand, decided that it was within the rules to go up to the child with the raised hand, hear her out, and then say something encouraging like, "Yes, I see why you wanted to ask me, but I'm sure you can think of a way to work it out on your own. Just do your best." This way, she explained, she would be pushing them along a little in a trouble spot instead of being so frighteningly mute.

Other teachers, after carefully reading the regulation books for their own tests, discovered that it was within the rules to talk to the children during the test as long as they weren't feeding them any answers. These teachers were free to remind kids, "Use the strategies we talked about in class" or "Remember to use the pace you found was best for you" or "Don't forget to follow the plan you made for taking the test—underlining or checking or using an index card to keep your place—whatever it was, use your plan." They were never telling the students answers, never telling them even particular strategies to use, they were only reminding them, in a general way, to do what they already knew they could do.

One teacher would do all this and more. As she walked around the classroom giving out these general reminders, she was also reassuring kids with back rubs, sending some out to have quick bathroom breaks, handing out sharp pencils, pouring juice, offering minidoughnuts, and generally cheerleading, "Hey kiddo! Hello-o-o! Test here, get crackin'!" or "Whoa, slow down, your head is going to break." She, like all the other teachers we talked to, had found the ways, within the confines of the rules, to help her students do the best they could.

Gathering Notes for Future Use

In talking to teachers about setting up the room, building a supportive context for kids, beginning the tests, and helping kids to use the strategies they know, it soon began to feel like there was nothing more any one teacher could do to support their students on test day. I mentioned this to one of the teachers I interviewed. "That may be true," she said, "but there are still things you can do to support them on the *next* test-taking day."

And she was right. Across the country, in the states where it was allowed, teachers we talked to were taking notes on the day of the test. Of course, for many teachers—for example, teachers in Texas—writing anything down during the timed testing period is currently not allowed. For others, however, the testing day is a once-in-a-year opportunity to gather data on how the kids actually function as they take the high-pressure reading test. Teachers who were permitted to take notes did so for a variety of reasons.

"I look over the kids' shoulders and jot notes to try to figure out some trends, like which questions a lot of kids got wrong, how far along most kids got before they lost their concentration, who got the really tricky ones right, things like that. The kinds of things the test companies don't explain when they send you the scores. Last year, I found out that every kid in my class had gotten the same one question wrong. The question had asked which event in the story probably took the longest. It made me realize that in the kids' book talks and in their test preparation, they rarely talk about time passing. It was an interesting new angle for us to take on in the classroom."

Other teachers took notes for entirely different reasons. "I take notes to use in parent conferences," one teacher explained. "I can tell them that halfway through the time, Annie's stamina was used up and she just couldn't concentrate anymore. Or that part of the reason that Kiron improved was probably his use of index cards throughout the test to help him block out distracting print."

Taking notes and recording facts like these can help parents understand the scores their children get, but most of all, can help us as teachers improve our test-proctoring practices and our test preparation practices for the next year. And the next year, and the next year, and the next.

Clearly, then, there are many decisions teachers must make for the day of the test. Some educators will create conditions to support standardization to the utmost—above and beyond what is called for by the regulations. Others will proctor according to the belief that, after the rules are satisfied, they bear the responsibility of making testing conditions as close to their students' natural learning environment as they possibly can. We've come to believe that whether we're arranging desks, setting a tone, or planning our teaching for the day, we have choices. Those choices will be determined not only by the regulations but also by our philosophies as educators.

10

The Politics of Reading Scores
and the Community

It was one of those achingly beautiful June mornings. The daffodils were out, radiant in the morning sunshine. The day felt blessed, and I felt blessed. Blessed with these beautiful children, laughing with delight as they swung hula hoops around their small hips, as their gala rings clattered down around their ankles. Blessed by the warmth of mothers, holding hands with their young scholars, pushing baby carriages full of promise. Inside the school's huge front foyer, I exchanged greetings with the security guard, signing my name and my institution's name with special flourish. It was that kind of day.

Then I turned the corner and walked into the school's front office. The door to the principal's office—to Tara's office—was closed. That door was *never* closed. Whenever I came to work with the teachers in this building, I'd head first into the warm bustle of Tara's office. I went there for the coat rack, sure, but mostly for the congeniality, the cup of coffee, the sense of shoulder-to-shoulder shared work. But today the door was closed; the dark wood, a stop sign in my face.

Mrs. Mattey said from her secretarial desk, "They're in a meeting." Instead of adding, "Go on in," she said, "Have a seat," and motioned for me to sit on the wooden bench where unruly children sit when they wait for their hearing. I sat and sat. After a time someone came over and whispered, "The scores are out."

Of course. Now it was clear. They were holed up with the scores. They were sitting with their hearts in their hands, learning what the Lord High Executioner had determined.

I knew how they felt, I knew what it was to hear, "The scores are here," and I knew about the quick scan job, the way one's heart leaps and falters to the tune of percentiles. I knew about the way daffodils and hula hoops disappear, dwarfed by The Computer Printout.

In every corner of every state, the scores come out in their own ways. Sometimes word trickles out first. "The district scores are in," people say out of the corners of their mouths, and everywhere people wait to see through the haze of whispered predictions, to see the concrete evidence of our individual culpability. Sometimes we get packets of individual scores, sometimes we get just the bare bones of percentiles, sometimes marginal jottings total the incline or decline of our children's scores, sometimes certain names or scores come circled in red.

The form in which the scores arrive varies, and the consequences vary even more. Across the nation, there are hundreds and thousands of tragic stories about the damage that has been caused by test scores. We all know of school districts ripped apart by competitiveness, backbiting, and hostilities that result from the scores' being better at one school than another, in one classroom than another. In some states, the scores a class or a school receives are translated into ratings, which carry with them implications for bonuses and job security. We all know of brilliant teachers who do not want to teach the children who most need them because those teachers don't want to be penalized if the children's scores aren't good. We all know of schools who arrange for their experienced teachers to teach the grades in which the kids will be tested, even at the cost of creating a leadership vacuum at other grade levels. We all know of principals whose tenure hangs on reading scores and who therefore invest every professional development dollar and every professional development day into teaching to the test. And no wonder.

When I was a child, my friends and I sometimes taunted each other by saying, "Sticks and stones may break my bones, but words will never hurt me." Now, as a grownup, I know that words, more than sticks or stones, can really hurt us. When schools and teachers are put on a "dishonor roll," the effect can be devastating. One of the problems with the labels based on test scores is that we accept them as the truth. We think that the damage is a consequence of the tests alone, but this is not true. The damage is also caused by people, and by people's responses to the tests. The devastation happens because of what people do in response to those test scores. And we human beings are very much in control of our responses to the hard things, including the hard test scores, that happen in our lives.

I was not always in control of my response to the test scores. For years and years, others would make the pronouncements about my scores. With fanfare, test scores would be announced and publicized. "Your scores went up, but less than those in the neighboring school." "For the second year in a row, your scores went down." "Your school is third—or thirtieth—in the city." Whatever the announcement was that day, I just lay down and took it. I took my children's scores and strapped them onto an arm band and wore them as part of my identity.

But since our study group's work with Ted, Jacqueline, and Beverly, things have been different. At one of our sessions with Ted and Jacqueline, we barraged them with questions about the hidden secrets of test success. We planned, in turn, to teach those secrets to our kids. But instead of teaching us the secrets of high scores, Ted and Jacqueline wanted to talk about scores.

One of us would say, "We went down again. By twelve points."

"Is that a raw score or percentile?" they'd respond.

"Who cares?" I'd wonder. "The point is we went down. We're in trouble. Big trouble."

Ted and Jacqueline may have sensed my impatience, but they nevertheless continued asking their statistical questions. They asked, "What do you mean when you say 'We went down?' Are you saying the *school's average* score went down? The *third graders'* average score went down? Or what?" They even asked what the percentiles meant. "If you went down 12 percentile points, how many fewer right answers was that? Out of a total of how many?"

I'm not a statistician. Nor have I ever wanted to be one. I just want to teach. And so I wanted to shoo away these pesky statistical questions and move on to the *real* issue of helping our children do better on the tests and of helping *us* as educators feel more responsible and trusted.

Then came Jasmine. I met Jasmine because, when our research team took on the challenge of interviewing and observing a group of fifth graders who were regarded as testing enigmas by their teacher, Jasmine was the child assigned to me. I first learned about her from her teacher, Don Fellman. "She's such a puzzle," he said. "If you had asked me, 'Who are your best readers?' I would have listed Jasmine, until I saw what the tests showed. I mean, in class she seems to have all the makings of a really good reader. She reads a ton, she says smart things in book talks. It's deceptive. In class, you get lulled into thinking she's a really strong reader. Then the tests come, and they show up her faults. She scored in the 71st percentile. So I know her reading isn't that strong. But to tell you the truth, I have no real sense of what her reading deficiencies are. I just know they're there."

How curious I was to meet Jasmine and to watch her taking a test. We settled ourselves into a corner, Jasmine, I, and Jacqueline, who was sharing in this day's field-based research. Before we asked Jasmine to take the test, we asked her to talk a bit about herself as a reader and as a test taker.

"I'm not that good of a reader," she said. "I'm a 71. My brother, when he was in fifth grade, was a 94. My brother is really smart." Then Jasmine went on to tell us about how she's not a good test taker and about how she's scared she won't get into college when she's older.

Ten minutes later, we gave Jasmine a practice CTB test, and settled down to watch. I was dazzled by what I saw. Clearly, Jasmine was a strong, thoughtful, rapid reader. She sat up straight, pulled the test close to her, and used her pencil as a pointer as she read the first passage, a short story. She read quickly and then turned her attention to the questions. The first question nudged her to flick her eyes back directly to a particular spot in the reading. This happened again on the second question. The third one gave her pause, and she scanned the text a bit before settling in to reread a part. I was stunned. How could it possibly be that this girl could have rated only in the 71st percentile?

I tried not to let my mind wander toward my questions. Jasmine was quietly progressing through the practice test, and I wanted to watch for where she slipped up. I read the passage along with her, hoping that would make me a keen observer. It was a story about a boy, Dave, who'd been accidentally locked in the basement. He had several broken clocks in his pocket and had spent his time tinkering with them. He eventually set off an alarm in one which ended up getting someone to unlock the basement door. The first question was about Dave's mood when he was in the basement with those clocks in his pocket: "Was Dave (A) amused, (B) frightened, (C) lonely, or (D) bored?"

I thought of Dave, with his pockets always full of those clocks. I pictured him tinkering with them, and I knew the answer: Dave was "(A) amused." Throughout the excerpt, Dave had struck me as the kind of person who loves to play with gadgets. And so I filled in my mental bubble. Just then, Jasmine reached out to circle "(A) amused." She explained her answer, "Because he liked to fix clocks," and I nodded in assent. She moved on to the next question. Then the answer sheet caught my eye. What? Could it be that Jasmine and I were both wrong? I checked again. The answer the test makers listed as correct was "(C) lonely." I couldn't believe my eyes. What evidence had there been that Dave was lonely? Alone, yes, but lonely? The evidence wasn't there.

Jasmine continued to dazzle me with her performance on the practice test. She got one other question wrong, out of carelessness, but otherwise her test was almost perfect. Later, when my colleagues and I met to talk over our enigmas, I wondered aloud about how she could have possibly received such a low score on the reading test.

Listening, Ted Chittenden asked, "So, she was in the 71st percentile? What was her *raw* score? How many wrong answers did she get?" I wanted to wave aside these detailed statistical considerations, but instead we dug out the computer printouts from the school office. They showed that children were rated at the 71st percentile if they answered twenty-eight questions correctly. Fine. There was the answer. Now, I was definitely ready to move on. But Ted was not.

"Twenty-eight correct? Out of how many?" he asked, still trying to understand how many questions Jasmine had answered incorrectly. But the total number of questions on the test wasn't shown on the computer sheets. We turned to go, needing to move on. And then we noticed that Sandra, in the same fifth-grade class, had been rated in the 91st percentile. We looked to see how many answers she had gotten right. She had answered *twenty-nine* questions correctly. Could that be? She got one more answer right than

Jasmine and scored 20 percentile points higher? We looked again. We had Ted look. Yes. Those were the facts. One question—one measly question—had made that kind of difference.

While I watched Jasmine, that very day, I had seen her using enormous intelligence, but getting a "wrong" answer. And to think that Jasmine's teacher and Jasmine herself had both let her score sway them from trusting their day-in, day-out evidence of Jasmine's strengths as a reader.

Jasmine's teacher and I spoke of how we wished we could scroll back time and relive the day when Jasmine's test scores had come, when Jasmine and her parents saw that she had earned a 71st percentile on the reading test. How we wished we could have sat with Jasmine and her parents and explained that just one more little correct answer would have given her an entirely different score. How we wished we could have explained the capriciousness of some of the test's questions and of the test's ways of assessing whether or not an answer was correct. It was upsetting that for a year now, Jasmine and her parents and her teacher had lived with an image of Jasmine as only an average reader whose strengths fall apart when the true test comes. And it was upsetting that in our ignorance we had let one score make us unsure of all the other evidence we had of Jasmine as a strong reader.

Knowledge Empowers

We could have altered the course of Jasmine's life if we'd been more informed about Jasmine's test scores. Test preparation can help children to be better prepared for tests, yes, but as teachers who live in a world of tests, we need to know not only how to prepare our children for tests but also how to read and respond to the test scores. We need to know how to read into and underneath and behind the scores, and we need to know what a person can and cannot conclude from these scores.

What a lesson I learned that day: Knowledge empowers.

If knowledge empowers, then it's no wonder that I have never felt empowered to author a response to test scores. It's no wonder that when the scores have come out, I have felt voiceless and unable to talk back to these scores. I was voiceless and powerless because I was ignorant. And I was not alone.

Among the members of our study group, it was astonishing how many didn't understand even the most fundamental things about reading test scores. Jasmine's situation helped me realize just how important it was to learn. Finally, I stopped seeing Ted and Jacqueline's questions as pesky and understood they were essential. How could I possibly learn from my children's test results and from my school's test results if I couldn't read the patterns that these scores revealed? Equally important, how could I help parents and the community interpret the scores if I myself didn't understand them?

Now I was ready to learn from Ted, Jacqueline, and anyone else who felt at home with stanines, percentiles, norming groups, and the like. I wanted to gulp down whatever insights I could and to try my hand at putting them to immediate use. From this point on, then, whenever Ted or Jacqueline asked one of their seemingly innocent questions about something we had said, I'd stop everything and ask, "Why do you ask that question? What are you getting at? Teach me your thinking."

I also wanted to invite others to learn with me. I wanted the teachers and principals with whom we worked to be able to take some control over the scores by having a greater knowledge of them. So my colleagues and I set up a Test Scores Hot Line for teachers and administrators to call with their questions about the test results. We let it be known that we were learning all we could about test scores and wanted anyone who was interested to learn with us.

Reading the Score Reports

It was four o'clock in the afternoon when the door to our office opened to three principals with whom we work closely. Each was carrying a huge stack of papers. They told me they had heard we were offering help and hoped that we would be able to help them make sense of their reports. They were worried. One principal told us his school was in jeopardy of becoming a SURR school—a School Under Registration Review, New York's designation for a low-performing school—if his school's scores weren't higher than last year.

I invited them into our library and watched them spread their papers across the table. It was overwhelming. There were pages and pages of information—scores reported for individual students, for each class, for the whole school. One principal even brought a report that broke down the scores according to the ethnicity of the students. I just looked at all of those pages and wondered how we would begin.

Luckily for us, Ted and Jacqueline were in the office that day. Who else but our ETS experts could help us understand the reports? I sat down at the table and pushed a pile of papers toward Ted. I leaned over my notebook, pen in hand, and waited for Ted to teach us. The room got very quiet. Ted's eyes flickered over the pages as if he'd never seen anything like them before. After a bit of time he looked up. I stared at him, ready to write down everything he said.

"How many questions were on the test? You've got a raw score here, but no total number of questions." Hmm. I looked down at the page, realizing his question was a wise one and waited for him to provide some understanding. Ted spoke again. "The report doesn't tell you which questions a child got correct and which they got incorrect. Is that information anywhere else?" I was perplexed. He kept asking more and more questions. I expected answers. Ted continued, "Is every question weighted the same? That is, are they worth the same number of points? Are the easier questions at the beginning of the exam weighted the same as later, harder questions? What kinds of scores are reported here—are these stanines, percentages, percentiles, or something else?"

By this time my mind was totally boggled. I'd been expecting Ted to clear up my confusion. Instead he'd raised whole new realms of uncertainty. I had never even thought to ask these questions. Until Ted asked, I never wondered whether different questions were worth a different number of points or what exactly the score columns meant. I was only interested in whether we went up or down and why. Yet, now, more than anything, my mind was boggled by the fact that Ted didn't seem to understand these forms any better than I did. "He works for ETS. They make the tests," I whispered to my friend. "And even he's confused?"

Later we looked over a pile of test scores with another testing expert, Claudia Gentile, from the Center for Performance Assessment. Once again I passed a score report to the expert, picked up a pen, and waited to be told what it meant. Watching Claudia was like watching someone open the back of a clock and study the gears. She held the page carefully, gliding her eyes across the entire thing. After quite some time spent musing over the page, Claudia looked up and spoke, "Okay, this is a reading test, and it's for fourth grade. Hmm. I wonder what the total number of items is? Is each question worth the same number of points?" Amazingly, Claudia responded to the report in much the same way as Ted and Jacqueline had—she raised more uncertainty. It was surprising to me that these three national experts on standardized testing would struggle through the reading of these reports. This time, however, instead of wondering privately, I came right out and asked Claudia about it. "You write the tests; why is it that when you read these forms you ask more questions than you answer?" Claudia explained, "I've looked at so many of these reports, each one so different from the next, that every time I begin, it's as if I know nothing and have to learn how to read them again. I've spent my career studying reading tests, but when I look at these reports I feel clueless and I have to orient myself to each one individually."

Later, as my colleagues and I reflected over the two years of our study, we realized that what Claudia had explained to us was important. It was all right to ask questions. The informed reader of tests is not somebody who knows all the answers but is somebody who asks the right questions. We knew this to be true in our work in reading and writing. The informed teacher is one who asks questions about what she sees her students doing as readers and writers in order to determine what they need to learn. So, too, questions are essential for reading score reports.

It was not, however, just that the testing experts asked questions but that they approached a score report as if it must have some internal logic, as if it would yield some helpful information with some work. From watching Ted and Claudia we've come to believe that there's a process for reading score reports that many test experts use. Claudia walked us through this process with one test report. As Claudia taught us how she made sense of a score report on a group of fourth graders who had taken the MEAP test, I took notes trying to name what she was doing in order to get a system we could all use another day with another score report.

Claudia's first piece of advice was to avoid reading the report from top to bottom as one would instinctively do, and to instead try to make sense of the categories of information presented on the sheet. This particular score report was entitled "Classroom Test Item Analysis," so Claudia and I knew we were looking at how students scored on individual items on the test. There were two basic divisions, "constructing meaning" items and "knowledge about reading" items. There was also a key in the middle of the page defining the three different types of "constructing meaning" items: "intersentence" questions required the reader to focus on small details of the text; "text" questions required the reader to attend to larger parts of the text; and "beyond the text" questions required the reader to integrate her own ideas into the text.

Next, we noticed that the scores were reported in two ways. First, for each item, the report showed the percentage of students who chose each possible response, with an asterisk next to the correct response. The second set of scores showed the frequency of correct scores for each type of question. We could see for individual classes how well kids had done on each type of question.

Then Claudia used the scores to try to answer particular questions about the school or about the group of children. Using this report, we wanted to know if the "intersentence" questions had been easier for the kids than the "beyond the text" questions. We suspected they had been. We turned to the scores, checking each item to see if the percentage of children with correct "intersentence" answers was greater that the percentage of children with correct "beyond the text" answers.

In the end, our guess was right, kids had scored higher on the "intersentence" questions. But that wasn't really the important part. What was important was the way we used scores to find out what we wanted to know, the way we felt empowered in reading them. By raising questions and focusing on them as we read, we could make new sense of the reports, and find new ways to talk about the scores.

Of course, we didn't totally trust the information we gleaned from the reports. Certainly, in the back of our minds we knew that what the test makers considered an "intersentence" error could really be an error of an entirely different sort. But for now we were only trying to see what the reports were saying. We also learned that we shouldn't feel that we needed to be alone as we analyzed the score reports. Gathering with a group of colleagues and talking through questions was very helpful.

In the following weeks, as more and more teachers and principals came to us with their score reports, we used what we had learned from Claudia, Ted, and Jacqueline to help them understand how the scores are reported.

When They Tell Us "The Scores Went Down"

The strategies we learned about reading the score reports became very useful when my friend and colleague Carol, a Reading Recovery–trained reading specialist at the City School called me in tears. Her school's scores had gone down. As if that wasn't bad enough, her principal had called Carol to her office. "I knew straight away something awful had happened," Carol said. Patricia, her principal, didn't invite Carol to take a seat on the sofa, and Patricia did not even leave the far side of her desk. "She just stood, glaring at me," Carol said. In a voice of steel, her principal had said, "I put my faith in you and your methods." She shoved the computer score sheets toward Carol and turned her back.

I met with Carol the next day, and we spent an hour with the score printouts. We pored over every detail, searching for redemption, or at least for illumination. At the start of the meeting, Carol was dazed, depressed, and passive. Half an hour later, she and I were perched on the edges of our seats, elbow-deep in our investigation, making headway.

The next day, Carol made an appointment to meet with her principal. "I need to show you something," she said. For the next half hour, Carol showed her principal that, in fact, there was *good* news as well as grim news.

When the district officials reported that the City School's scores had gone down, they were looking at the fact that this year 14 percent of the school's third graders had not reached the 50th percentile. Since last year only 6 percent had not reached that percentile, this showed a decline. Obviously this was a concern. But, meanwhile, the number of children in the bottom quartile, those who scored in the 25th percentile and below, had decreased dramatically. Most of those readers had moved up and were now receiving scores in the 25th–35th percentile range. These students who had demonstrated such progress had in fact been the students with whom Carol had worked.

This information changed the way we thought about looking at the scores for many schools. Instead of looking only at how the scores fall in relation to the 50th percentile, it seemed more helpful to examine how scores fall out in quartiles: 0–25th percentile; 25–50th percentile, and so on, thus showing how particular subgroups of students moved. Additionally, reporting in relation to the 50th percentile not only leads to problems like those faced by Carol, but also has some ramifications that can be quite damaging to some students. It could lead, for example, to policies that advocate marshaling efforts of the school predominantly toward those students who, with some effort, will be able to score at or above the 50th percentile, with those who are not in shooting range of crossing that all-important passing line ending up without the supports they need to improve.

For Carol, this information was important in that it helped the principal regain faith in her methods. Carol had now learned that she need not be the passive recipient of whatever interpretation anyone might care to give. "Any other year, I would have put my tail between my legs," Carol said. "I would have slunk out of there in shame. But this time we were able to look more closely at the scores and to see other stories, other information contained in them."

In the days to come, more calls came in from teachers and principals who had been told that their scores had gone down. Now, instead of accepting that as a given, we knew we could look at the scores ourselves. We learned that when the district office shows us the numbers and tells us our scores, we need to ask which numbers they are looking at, and which numbers they are using for comparison. We need to say, "Okay, now look at it *this* way." There are many different stories in a score report.

Over the next few weeks we were able to analyze the scores in many different ways. In one school, the district office defined the scores as going down because the school's *rank* in the district had gone down. And yet, in this school, the percentage of students who scored at or above the 50th percentile had increased dramatically from the previous year. It just so happened that this had occurred at the other schools in the district as well.

In another district, schools were also ranked in order of test scores. The highest-ranking schools were celebrating their great successes, and the lowest-ranking schools were cowering and reassessing themselves. All over the district, reputations were being defined. We compared the scores of the highest and lowest schools to find out how much of a difference there really was between them. We discovered that the difference in the number of children being at or above the 50th percentile was very small. Statisticians told us that it was like trying to say there was a significant difference in age between children born September 1st, 3d, and 5th of the same year. The ranking emphasized differences in scores that were really very small. The principals in this district would need to find other reasons to celebrate or cower.

To Whom Are My Kids Being Compared?

One day, our hot line received a call from principal Colleen Peña from P.S. 556. The staff of the district office had commended her for her children's scores overall but was concerned about the number of children scoring in the bottom quartile, below the 25th percentile. In the district's estimation, even though the overall scores for the building were strong, there were still too many students who were doing poorly on the test, and the district office staff questioned the school's reading program. They believed that the school's method for teaching reading was fine for strong readers but not for kids who were struggling. The staff compared Colleen's school to another school in the district with a different reading program and told her that the struggling kids were doing better in that other school. Colleen didn't believe that it was the reading program in her school that was causing some students to do poorly, but she didn't know what to say back to the district office. Later, I visited her school in order to think with her about what could account for the higher number of kids scoring in the bottom quartile in her school.

As we walked around her building, Colleen explained to me that her school had a gifted program as well as a regular program. Each grade had two general education classes and a gifted class. The gifted program didn't function as an active, strong magnet for the district. That is, it wasn't filled with kids from around the district but only with kids from her school. I realized that the gifted program had the effect of depleting the general education classes of some of its strongest students. If the school were to draw its gifted program from a larger population, say the entire district or the city, there would be more chance that above-average students would stay in the regular classes. Instead, students who were doing well ended up moving into the gifted classes. This could be the reason why the kids who scored in the bottom quartile continued to score there instead of moving up. This gifted program had in effect created tracking, had created general education classes that weren't as heterogeneous as they'd otherwise be. And research has shown that this isn't helpful to those in the lower track, when there isn't the full diversity of intellect.

Another factor that may have influenced the distribution of scores in this school was that because only a limited number of gifted children were available to fill the gifted classes, some strong, hard-working, average-scoring students were pulled into the gifted program, thus depleting the regular classes of even more of the better-scoring students. Once they were in the gifted classes, the very respectable scores of these students were no longer regarded as an accomplishment: "Oh well, these kids are gifted."

When I left that day, both Colleen and I felt we had a new understanding of which realities her test scores were reflecting. She wasn't about to abandon her gifted program because there were other reasons for it. But she also wasn't ready to alter her reading program as if it were the sole culprit behind the lower quartile scores. She was now ready to respond to the district office staff complaints. The scores were not necessarily reflecting a problem with the reading program.

How Are the Scores Compared?

Colleen's wasn't the only phone call we received about a school whose methods were in question because of test scores. Mitchell Pierce called with the same problem. He had spent the last year researching literacy education methods and applying this research to his methods of teaching reading. And then the test scores came back. Mitchell's principal left a message in his mailbox saying they needed to talk. Mitchell's scores had gone down six points, and the principal blamed his methods.

The first thing Mitchell and I talked about was that six points is not a statistically significant difference. I reminded him of what Ted Chittenden and Jacqueline Jones had taught us about score deviations. That is, if a child were to take two equivalent tests, the scores the child received on the two tests might be strikingly different. The difference between those two scores is described as statistically insignificant. Ted and Jacqueline had told us that their colleagues at Educational Testing Service (the publisher of the SAT exam and other tests) would not think that a small dip in reading scores revealed anything. In fact, both of them explained that most scores would be most accurately reported in bands. That is, if a student scored in the 64th percentile on a test, the most accurate way to report that score would probably be within a band of scores, say, 58th–88th percentile. One type of score that represents a band is called a stanine score. Stanine scores spread the raw scores onto a scale of one to nine (hence the name—standard nine), thus allowing for more overlap in students' scores and eliminating the illusion of significant differences between students who are equivalent.

The second issue that Mitchell and I discussed was that his principal had calculated that his scores had gone down six points by comparing Mitchell's fourth graders this year to his fourth graders last year. In doing this, he was ignoring the fact that these were different students taking different tests. How could anyone claim that Mitchell's teaching methods are *the* variable that caused the scores to go down when both the students and tests were different? It would be more reasonable to compare the scores Mitchell's students earned this year to their scores last year as third graders. In fact, when anyone wants to draw conclusions about instruction by interpreting test scores, examining the scores of a single group of students over time is the one accepted way to do it. This is called plotting longitudinal cohort groups. Of course, one has to take into account changing school populations (which can amount to 30, 50, or even 80 percent turnover in the course of a school year), so this is best done with groups or classes that experience little or no transience.

As for Mitchell, we looked at the history of his current fourth graders to try to see what we could about their low scores and discovered that, in fact, this was a group that had consistently contained more struggling readers than his previous group. Furthermore, as first graders, one class had spent most of the year with substitute teachers. As third graders, that class had been housed in the gymnasium because of overcrowding in the school. Therefore, if there is any need to explain lower scores this year, there are many possible explanations besides the change in Mitchell's teaching methods.

My Kids Can't Get the Main Idea

A fax came into my office one morning from Missouri. Attached was a test score report and a note that said, "They told me my kids can't figure out the main idea of a story." The fax had come from Pam Geller, a teacher who had joined our study group. Pam had received this message from her district office and was dumbfounded. "What do they mean, my kids can't find the main idea of a story? We talk about main ideas all the time in our reading. How can that be?"

Pam and I looked at the score report. On it was the percentage of students in the third grade who had mastered each of the eighteen skills defined by the test. As we went through the report we noticed something very strange. It seemed that while only 29 percent of the third graders had mastered the "Main Idea," 56 percent had mastered "Generalizations." What was the difference, in the test makers' minds, between "Main Idea" and "Generalizations"? As we looked further, we found more skills that appeared to be similar to one another. There was a skill defined as "Story Title." From our research we knew that the way the test writers often asked the students to find the main idea of a passage was to have them choose among a list of possible story titles. Yet on this test, these were separate skills. What was the difference? And what made the kids do better on one than the other?

We were puzzled. We knew we wouldn't be able to go back to the test to find out why the children had answered the particular questions the way they had, so we decided to go back to our notes from researching the kids as test takers to see if we could draw any conclusions. Pam went back to notes she had collected from watching kids take practice tests from a booklet that claimed its questions tested particular skills. We were reminded of what we had discovered at the time about how kids choose their answers. Usually, kids choose wrong answers for completely different reasons than official test analyzers suggest. For example, one practice passage with which Pam worked read something like this:

> Ancient Egyptians built monuments to honor their rulers. A sphinx has a human head and a lion's body. The oldest and biggest sphinx is called the Great Sphinx. It was made in the desert in Egypt many thousands of years ago. The Great Sphinx is sometimes buried under sand, and some of the stone has been worn away by rough weather. Today scientists are trying to preserve the Great Sphinx.
>
> Question: What kind of land surrounds the Great Sphinx?
>
> A   snowy
> B   dry
> C   rainy
> D   full of trees

Choosing an incorrect answer here, according to the test makers, indicates children's inability to "apply background knowledge" to their reading. For this question, applying background knowledge would mean that the child, knowing the Sphinx was in Egypt in a desert, would think of what he knows of Egypt and deserts and choose the answer to match his knowledge—the land there is "(B) dry." In Pat's class, however, one child got the question wrong because, having just immigrated from a different country and curriculum, he had never before heard of Egypt or deserts and didn't know what the land was like there. Instead, he thought of weather from his homeland that would be strong enough to wear away stone, and applying his experience, he chose "(C) rainy." Although his answer was wrong, he had applied his background knowledge with expertise—the test had failed to test accurately for this skill.

In her book *With Literacy and Justice for All* (1991), Carole Edelsky cites other examples of questions that test things other than reading. Sometimes students answer questions incorrectly because they don't have the factual information required for the questions. For example, "The frequency of a sound determines its: treble, pitch, volume, or harmony." Other times students choose incorrect answers because their experiences differ from those of the test maker. For example, students without experience with peach trees will probably be troubled by the question "If you picked all the peaches off a peach tree, would the tree die? Yes or No?"

Knowing that there is often little or no correlation between the real reasons kids get answers wrong and the test makers' reasons why kids get answers wrong has been very important. Again and again people from district offices or test publishers have analyzed test results and then mandated curricular emphases based on the skills they have found kids lacking. District office memos were being handed out by the sackful describing to teachers the particular skills that were tested, with examples of questions for each one. Often this entire enterprise is built upon incorrect assumptions about the reasons why children answer some questions incorrectly.

Uh-Oh, My Test Scores Went Up

I recently visited a school in which the front foyer of the building displayed huge bar graphs, plotting the upward progress of the school's test scores. Above the bar graph was a lavish sign saying, "We're on the move," and indeed the scores had risen dramatically. Now the school was preparing to take a new state test. I was in the building because my colleagues and I were about to begin staff development work with the school's entire staff. Standing before the display in the front hallway, I felt my heart sink. "Oh, no," I thought, "there's going to be trouble."

My anxiety came because I could already read the writing on the wall. We were going to work with teachers for a few months, and then the kids would take the new test and the test results would be lower. What would the principal display in her front hallway then?

I was quite certain that scores would go down because they generally do go down when a school takes a new test. This is because the school is not familiar with or practiced on the new test. But even without the fact of the new test, the hallway display worried me. It is just as likely that scores will go down as that they will go up. Sometimes scores fluctuate for no reason at all. A five-point drop in scores is meaningless. But when the school building has made such a huge deal of its progress on test scores, it won't be easy to explain any drop at all.

My first bit of advice to the principal was to remove the display. I then told her that it is common knowledge that when schools switch tests, the scores generally go down. If her scores are high, not talking about it will just make people think she's being humble, but meanwhile she'll just protect herself for when the inevitable happens and her scores dip.

Meanwhile, while most of the calls to our hot line were from teachers and administrators concerned because their scores had gone down, we also received a couple of calls from people whose scores had gone up. One such call came from Allison Marks, a fifth-grade teacher. Allison told us that last year she had focused most of her attention on her reading program, trying to improve her methods of instruction. When the scores came back, everyone in the district praised her for her students' increase in scores. The district office crowned her Teacher of the Year and asked her to be a mentor teacher for her school, hoping she would help other teachers raise their test scores as well.

Allison was terrified. Not only was she unsure of how to help the other teachers in her building improve their scores, she was panicked that she would not repeat her success. What if her scores dropped this year? For Allison and teachers like her, it was critical that she not let the district draw conclusions from the good years any more than from the bad years. What goes up will come down. There will be years of high scores and years of low. What is most important, however, is that the years not be compared. Allison and her colleagues in her district need to remember that this is a new group of students achieving the new and higher scores. Allison needs to remind people that one group of students can't be compared to the next as if the groups are exactly the same, because when we're dealing with small numbers (like the population of a school or a classroom), *it's not true* that "the differences average out."

High test scores do, however, provide particular opportunities for teachers. When our scores are high, we can criticize the test and people will listen to us. When our scores are low, it is almost impossible to avoid sounding defensive if we point out that tests are a one-day-only measurement, that they aren't testing many of the skills we most value, or that one year's class of students can't be contrasted with others. When our scores are up, however, we're in a great position to say all of this.

I Switched to a New Test and My Scores Still Went Down

One of the hardest issues we faced was when Diane Mathis called from a Midwestern town to tell us her surprising news—her test scores had gone down. You see, the teachers in Diane's school had been involved in a state-funded project to rethink the teaching of reading in their school. The entire staff was involved in the project, and teachers were working day and night, meeting during preparation periods, early in the morning and after school, to think about their reading instruction. They studied in courses together and read professional literature together. The administration had tried to find a test that was more closely aligned to the school's beliefs about reading and had given that test in addition to the required test. Everyone was sure that the scores would be high on the new test, reflecting both the improved teaching of reading and the improved test.

But the scores still came back low. Everyone was depressed. How could it be that a test that was supposed to be more closely aligned with the way the teachers taught could still show low scores? Were the kids really only average as readers? First, we told Diane that it is probably wrong to expect that a switch in tests will show higher scores instantaneously. When a new test is introduced, scores go down at first and then rise in succeeding years as students and teachers become more used to it.

Next, we explained that we had learned that when a new test is developed, the test makers have to field-test it in order to measure its validity. One common way to measure a test's validity is to compare its results with other established tests' results. If the scores on the new test are quite different from those on the established test, the new test is likely to be considered not valid. On the other hand, if children who scored in the 80th percentile on the new test also scored in the 80th percentile on the old test, then the new test is apt to be regarded as valid. Because of this, it is unlikely that the new test that Diane's school chose would produce very different scores than the old test would. The new test had to show comparable scores overall, or it would have been discarded as invalid.

And yet schools and districts need to search for new tests that are more closely aligned with their beliefs. So what can they do? The first action is to be informed of the quality of the test under consideration. One good place to turn is the *Mental Measurements Yearbook* (*MMY*). Found in most major libraries, the *MMY* provides easy-to-read descriptions of a multitude of large-scale assessments and can help educators choose tests that are both valid and reflective of their beliefs about good education.

We also told Diane about instances in cities we know well where the state-of-the-art schools that are clearly light-years ahead of other schools in a discipline (writing, math) *don't* come out on the very top scorewise. We knew of several instances where these schools pulled in very respectable, but not superlative, scores. The plain truth is, true excellence and rigor show up more in long-term projects, such as examples of student work, than in top-flight scores.

My District Is Demanding Impossible Goals

In the course of working on the hot line, I learned that the New York City goal of having all children reading on grade level (defined as scoring at or above the 50th percentile) is an almost impossible goal to reach. At first, I thought it was impossible because norm-referenced tests are designed so that, if graphed, the scores must fall into a bell curve, meaning that half the students will score above the 50th percentile and half will score below. While this is true, the tests aren't being normed by a group of students whose demographics are like those of my students. Neither an exclusively urban nor an exclusively suburban population tends to match the national norming populations because this latter group assumes a testing population that includes *both* urban and suburban populations. This is to say, my urban schools have higher proportions of poor students and higher proportions of linguistic diversity than does the population in the national norming group. Because children in these schools had less access to books and had larger classes, and because, as we have already learned, most tests are biased against these groups, it is highly unlikely that all students in urban populations will score above the national norms. Schools would do well to find out as much as they can about the norming population of their test. Teachers and administrators should be able to find out this information by calling the toll-free number on the inside of their test booklets.

I recently heard about a major, well known national test in which urban students were being compared to a sampling of other urban students. While this is meant to compare similar students, it creates problems in that it suggests two tiers of educational expectations. On the other hand, in our society of haves and have nots we have a two-tier system of opportunity. A recent *New York Times* article reported that students in the city were still doing poorly as compared to the rest of the state. And then, in the same newspaper, Sandra Feldman, president of the American Federation of Teachers, reported in her weekly column that despite conclusive evidence that smaller class sizes affect student achievement, poor students in inner city schools are often crowded into classes of thirty, thirty-five, and even forty students. (March 8, 1998)

The fact that reading on grade level means scoring at the 50th percentile on nationally normed tests is problematic for other reasons. People have more than once phoned us to say, "I just learned that 30 percent of the children in my city are reading below grade level. We're in a crisis situation. What should we do?" My response has been to tell them that they should feel okay. This is not a crisis. It means that 70 percent of students are reading above grade level on a test that is designed for only 50 percent of students to do so. Similarly, parents sometimes call in a state of total alarm because they've learned that their child is reading "below grade level." The child may, however, be reading at the 46th percentile, which is just about average for her class. It would be more helpful to say that "reading on grade level" means reading in the average range, which could be defined as anywhere between the 30th and 70th percentiles.

Across the country school systems are setting other goals or sanctions that are problematic as well. In many districts there is a move to withhold diplomas based on test scores. Some experts say that this consequence will bring a rise in "opportunity to learn" lawsuits against the school system. Parents and children will sue stating, "How can you withhold my diploma when my math teacher is teaching without proper certification and when we know as a fact that a student's ability to perform well has much to do with class size and the number of books per child?" In *The Literacy Crisis,* Jeff McQuillan cites data showing that the average child living in Beverly Hills has two hundred books in her home, while in neighboring Watts there is an average of twenty-four books per child in the school (McQuillan, 1998). How can students with substandard opportunities be held accountable to high test scores?

There Are So Many Different Types of Scores

As the weeks went by, and my colleagues and I read through more and more score reports, we realized that another important thing to understand is that there are so many different kinds of scores. What do they all mean, and which ones should we pay closest attention to? There seem to be two general categories of scores. The first are scores that are familiar, the typical statistical scores. They are the ones we've mentioned often in this book: percentiles, which compare students to one another; raw scores, which show the number of items on a test a student got correct; stanines, which represent the raw scores in a band of one to nine. The second category of scores are those that are created for a particular test. For example, in Texas students receive a Texas Learning Index. In Michigan students receive a test score of approximately 215–360 for each of the two passages in the MEAP test, which is then translated to a performance measure—"satisfactory," "moderate," or "low." Another type of customized score is the one the *New York Times* invented to show citywide reading scores adjusted for particular issues deemed important to consider when comparing students. The *Times* took into account issues of poverty, number of children receiving free lunch, attendance, and so on.

Besides understanding which category of scores we're reading, we need to know, first and foremost, how the scores are reported. Often, scores are reported in one way to one constituency and another way to another constituency. For example, in New York City, the reports that teachers receive include percentiles, raw scores, normal curve equivalents, and often a state reference point rating of "above," "far above," or "below." The reports parents receive, however, only contain the percentile score. There is no raw score that could show how many items the child got correct; just the comparison to the norming group is shared.

Second, for those of us who use customized scores, it is important, although difficult, to find out as much as possible about how the scores were created. I say "difficult" because stories abound of teachers and administrators trying to gather information about their scores only to realize it's impossible. For example, in Michigan, one can read the entire MEAP handbook to the score reports and never find any information pertaining to how the test score was created. And in New York City, few people truly understand how the *Times* created the formula for the scores it invented.

No matter what scores are reported, there is certain information that schools and we, as teachers, should find out. When looking at raw scores, we should be sure to know the total number of items on the test. This is important because it helps us figure out what percentage of the test a student had to get correct in order to be at a particular percentile and therefore puts some perspective on the percentiles. For example, one student we researched answered forty out of fifty questions on his reading test correctly (80 percent of the questions answered correctly) and yet received a percentile score of 49. Additionally, we should always know the range of scores for a group of students as well as how the scores are spread around the average score. That is, are students' scores crowded around the average, or were there lots of highs and lots of lows? Two schools might learn that the average score their students received was at the 63d percentile. For one of these, the scores might all fall in the 50th–70th percentile range. For the other school, the children might be divided between both the bottom and top quartiles, with almost no one scoring in the midrange. A school's response to its scores would differ depending on the distribution of the scores.

My Kids Aren't Proficient Readers

In the course of learning about the different types of scores that are reported to schools and parents, it became clear to us that while we agreed that reporting the scores in bands was better than reporting them in percentiles because the former tends to do away with false differences between readers, there were, in fact, problems with bands as well. The first problem with chunking kids into larger categories of readers lies in how the cutoffs for those categories are determined. We wondered how it was decided, for example, what raw score a student would need in order to be considered a satisfactory reader on the MEAP test.

In her book *With Literacy and Justice for All* (1991), Carole Edelsky brings home the point of the arbitrariness of cutoff points by describing how passing grades for the National Teaching Exam (NTE) are determined in Delaware. Edelsky explains that in Delaware the score a prospective teacher needs to receive in order to pass the NTE varies according to the demand for teachers in the marketplace. The more teaching positions that need to be filled, the lower the score needed to pass the exam.

Another problem with these categories of reading is in the names often used to describe them. One teacher with whom we worked told us the story of a parent who was quite upset that her child was not reading at the "satisfactory" level for her test. The parent didn't know that "satisfactory" was the name for the category of readers who scored highest on the test. The name of the category made it seem as if her child could not read at all. Similarly, as tests change in schools and school districts, so do the categories of readers. In this way, a family with three children might find that the youngest child is given an entirely different determination as a reader than the other two children without realizing that the difference is as likely to be in category names as it is in reading abilities.

Whose Scores Are Included in the Score Reports?

It is important to know *how* the scores are reported, but it is equally important to know *whose* scores are reported. Schools receive scores in a variety of ways. Sometimes the scores are divided by district, school, class (subgroup of students), or individual students. This process of separating out scores of different populations is known as disaggregating the scores, and it is used in a variety of ways.

Sometimes decisions about how scores are disaggregated are to the detriment of students. In some communities, in the name of showing higher scores, particular populations of students are excluded from the reports. Very often the excluded students are those in special-education programs or those who are English Language Learners (ELL). To exclude their scores, some districts even exempt these children from taking the tests. With respect to English Language Learners, Monty Neil, Director of Fair Test, points out that this issue is complicated by the fact that standardized reading tests are often totally inappropriate for these students and can cause them harm with totally invalid results.

Excluding scores has a particularly damaging effect for some children, namely those predicted to score poorly, in that some are placed in special-education classes so that they won't have to take the tests and their scores won't be included in the reports (Darling-Hammond, 1991). Additionally, there are other consequences to how scores are disaggregated. These include retaining students in grades so that their relative standing will look better on "grade-equivalent" scores, excluding low-scoring students from admissions to "open enrollment" schools, and encouraging low-scoring students to drop out (Darling-Hammond, 1991; Shepard, 1989).

Disaggregating the scores can also prove useful. For example, often advocates for educational equity will separate out the scores by particular populations to see if there is any evidence of problems in equitable educational opportunities as shown by a split in test scores by particular groups of students.

We as teachers should know not only how the scores in our communities are disaggregated but where the pressure is coming from for the scores to be disaggregated that particular way. We often take it as a given that scores show up the way they do, but it is important to know that decisions about how scores are reported may reflect particular goals external to the classroom, and that they can benefit or harm certain groups of students, teachers, or schools. In one Midwestern state, doing well on the test has to mean not only that the school does well on average but that all the different populations of students are shown to be doing well. In this way, the school does not let the high scores of some parts of the school's population hide the poor performance of other parts.

We may want to find out if the scores can be disaggregated for us, or we may disaggregate the scores ourselves to be able to talk about the scores in a variety of ways. For example, one school with which we worked disaggregated their scores by the number of years students had been in the school. They found that the students who had been in the school for three or more years were doing fine on the test. Schools might also disaggregate the scores by other subpopulations of students, for instance those receiving the services of the reading teacher. This is what Carol did at the City School to show that the scores of the students they were paying particular attention to had, in fact, gone up.

When we began our test preparation work, our hope was to help our kids get higher scores. We took those scores and the way they were reported as givens. If the district told us our kids were doing poorly, we accepted it as fact. Through our hot line, we have learned that with knowledge, we can tell the stories of our scores differently. We learned that instead of lying down and taking the news, we could ask questions—about how the scores are determined and who is included. We could draw our own conclusions about the scores our children receive. We learned that we could author the stories of the scores.

11

Taking Our Place at the Policy Table

I read too many children's books: How I yearn for a "happily ever after" ending! I want the dove to return bearing a fig leaf. I want the puppy to be born, or the new prince. I want to glimpse the Promised Land against the horizon. I want the sun to set, casting a golden glow over the world. I want the satisfaction of a happy ending. How sorry I am that the sun cannot set and that I cannot give my readers a glimpse of the Promised Land. Instead, this book ends at high noon in the midst of a blazing drama.

The drama occurs on a national and international stage. The players include politicians, gigantic corporate conglomerates, the media industry, and teachers' unions and professional organizations. It is easy to feel that we are the little guys, the pawns, underlings at the mercy of forces far bigger than us. It is tempting to duck inside our classrooms, to close our doors tightly against the hurricane-like winds of change that swirl about us, winds generated in part by the machine of norm-referenced, multiple-choice exams and by the increasingly high stakes attached to test scores.

But of course, shouldering our weight against our closed classroom doors doesn't shut out the effects of the tests. These effects are already within our classrooms and within our souls. Most of us struggle daily, caught in a tug-of-war between what we as professionals value and what we know is valued on the tests that are the sole measuring stick rating us and our students. At graduate schools of education such as the one to which we belong—Teachers College, Columbia University—and at professional conferences across the globe, we are taught to go to great lengths to support collaboration, thoughtfulness, inquiry, revision, choice, craftsmanship, and student investment in our classrooms. Yet our children are usually assessed through tests that do not put a premium on any of this. We are torn between a belief that our children should write essays, prepare for debates, and pursue long-term projects and the brutal reality that none of this counts in the great ledger of norm-referenced, multiple-choice reading exams. Across the hall, children in another classroom spend their time coloring in bubbles and filling in the blanks. We do not understand a profession that talks the talk of valuing what we do, and then, on Judgment Day, forsakes us. We feel confused, deceived, and undermined.

What, then, are we to do? We are the little guys in this drama, and we are up against forces that feel all-powerful and unavoidable. What are we to do?

We have reached the place in this story—in the story of this book and in the story of the profession—where it's time for the music to change, for the narrator's intonation to shift, for the problem posing to be behind us. It is time to turn the page and to have the story shift. It is time to read "One day . . . , " it is time for an unlikely character to step forward and to do something or to suggest something that changes everything. In this story, that character will not be the traveling minstrel, the young lad with an answer to the king's riddle, or the youngest sister emerging from her place at the hearth.

In this story, we must be the characters who step forward. It is time for classroom teachers to draw our chairs up to the policy table. It is time for us to have a voice in shaping the standards and the measures of assessment that so powerfully direct our profession. It is time for each of us to come out from behind our classroom door, to step forward as a major player in this drama.

"But, but, but . . ." some may sputter.

I know the feeling. I voiced the same protest at the thought of writing this book, at the notion that I might join the conversation about standardized tests. We know full well that decisions about state and national assessments have been in the hands of politicians, state education commissioners, boards of education, and publishers. This isn't our arena. I, for one, feel more at home sitting alongside Malik, listening to him read a page from *Boxcar Children*. I squirm at the idea of being part of policy decisions about standardized tests, and I know many readers are squirming along with me.

"I am just the little guy in this," we protest. "I am just a class-room teacher." But even as we sputter our protest, we already know that it is absolutely, totally obvious that teachers need to have stronger voices in this conversation. We understand education because we are on the front lines of it. We make the countless minute-by-minute decisions that are absolutely essential in the lives of children and their families. We need to coauthor, to understand, and to affirm the contexts and expectations within which we teach.

There has never been a more important time for teachers to come forth and claim our place at the policy table. It is important to realize that the increased stakes that politicians and others have put into norm-referenced, multiple-choice tests are part of a trend in national politics to pin the world's problems onto schools, and then to suggest that the solution to those problems lies either in using the big stick of sanctions for low test scores or else legislation to wrest control of schools away from educators. Across the nation, one can see evidence of a concerted effort to take control of teaching—especially of the teaching of reading—out of teachers' hands. It is no accident that the hyped focus on test scores comes just as, for example, in the trend-setting state of California the state legislature is passing laws telling teachers how to teach emergent readers, which books can and cannot go in our classroom libraries, and how we are to work with children whose first language is not English. California legislators are even controlling professional literacy workshops for teachers. It is now the law that workshops paid for with state funds must feature a 75 percent focus on phonemic awareness and decoding strategies.

In children's books, when an unlikely character steps forward and turns the tide of events, those characters inevitably do this by relying on their wits. If we are to make a significant contribution to testing and assessment policies in our schools and our nation, we, too, need to our to rely on our wits. We need to read the terrain so that our contributions will be judicious and well-timed.

We need to begin by realizing that the forces behind standardized assessment are significant. The call for large-scale, standardized measures of assessment is not likely to go away soon. Once upon a time, I used to speak out against all standardized reading tests, claiming that assessment belonged in the hands of classroom teachers. Now, I would no longer waste my energy on that battle. As long as schools receive state and federal funding, there will be efforts made to compare student achievement based on standardized forms of measurement.

The tests won't go away but they can be far less damaging to us and to our children. Our voices can make the difference. Sometimes I think those of us who are uncomfortable with standardized exams try to look the other way from the tests, ignoring them entirely out of our distaste for them. This isn't wise. The tests exert too big an influence on our lives and our profession for us to continue to play ostrich. We can help to influence the development and selection of tests, realizing that all tests are not created equal. We can also raise our voices and cast our votes toward creating wiser policies for interpreting and making decisions based on test scores. We might consider supporting the National Center for Fair & Open Testing (Fair Test), the only national organization working exclusively to end the overuse and misuse of standardized multiple-choice tests. Fair Test is a network that can provide information, technical assistance, and advocacy on testing concerns. For the remaining pages of this chapter, I want to urge readers to speak out for a handful of particularly important and possible causes.

Become Advocates for Criterion-Referenced, Standards-Based, Performance Assessments

First, I believe we need to speak out against the fact that many of our states continue to give norm-referenced rather than criterion-referenced tests. It doesn't have to be this way. There are plenty of examples around of criterion-referenced tests. If ETS can produce both the norm-referenced SAT exam and the criterion-referenced Advanced Placement (AP) exam, this suggests they and other vendors could produce criterion-referenced reading tests for us all.

Let me explain why this issue merits our attention. Let us consider, for a moment, the differences between the Advanced Placement and the SAT exams. Secondary school students who take AP exams in particular disciplines know in advance what each test will cover. They know that if they work hard in school, if they study and perform well, the chances are great that there will be a payoff for them when they take the exam. The purpose of this and other criterion-referenced tests, then, is to hold teachers and students to a clearly-articulated standard. The test scaffolds instruction.

On the other hand, secondary school students who take the SAT exam know that their schoolwork will *not* be tied to that test. If they do well in their courses of study at school, this has no bearing on the test. And if they receive high scores on the SAT exam, their success probably reflects their background knowledge and vocabulary, which would indicate that the best route to success on the SAT exam is to grow up in an educated home.

I believe the purposes behind the two kinds of exams are altogether different, and I vastly prefer the purposes of the AP exams (brought down to the level of our children and designed to support the curriculum of our reading workshops) rather than the purposes of SAT exams (which are very similar to the current norm-referenced reading tests given to millions of children each year).

Let me back up. As I see it, there are some reasonable motivations and some very bad motivations behind the current frenzy over reading tests. If I want to give politicians and the public the benefit of the doubt, I'll assume that their interest in test scores grows out of the same idealistic, far-reaching goals for children that my colleagues and I aim for. That is, I will assume that the current emphasis on test scores comes from a determination to make sure we, as a nation, are helping every child from every town and city reach her full potential. The tests, then, become important because they give politicians, the public, and us, as educators, ways to look at inclining and declining trends in student achievement across different states and cities, across rich and poor communities. This is a reasonable purpose, and criterion-referenced exams can play a role in this mission. Our hope would be, in designing these tests, that if we are clear about what is necessary for students to know and to be able to do, more and more students will eventually do well on the tests.

But often there are very different purposes driving tests. There is a long historical tradition in the United States of using standardized tests as a way to divide children into the winners and the losers. Norm-referenced tests like the SAT exam have been carefully designed to guarantee that the scores young people earn will be dispersed as on a bell curve. The SAT exam, then, allows the educational system to track students into different categories of higher education. Because norm-referenced tests are designed so that people are always distributed along a bell curve with only a few people earning very high scores, these tests designate an elite and enable us to then give special opportunities to students who are regarded as the "best and the brightest."

It is arguable that by the time children are sixteen, this might be a reasonable thing to do. But it seems to me that it would be contrary to the purposes of schooling to, for example, give a child's version of the SAT exam to six-year-old children, then to derive scores from these exams, and to admit only the high-scoring children into the finest levels of elementary school. The purpose of school should be to give all children the opportunity to work hard and to achieve. A child needn't already be smart when he arrives at school's doorstep. Instead, school is meant to be the place you come to in order to get smart.

Because norm-referenced reading tests are specifically designed (like the SAT exams) to ensure that half of those who take the tests always and inevitably fail, when states persist in giving children norm-referenced reading tests this says to me that the state wants a way to sort children, teachers, and schools into winners and losers. And I question why this is helpful. Tests that do this are *not* about the business of clarifying and holding us all to high expectations. Instead, they are about finding tricky ways to ensure that many, many children and teachers fail. When people argue that tests such as these "hold teachers accountable," I respond that on the contrary, it seems to me that most norm-referenced tests accomplish just the opposite.

A second reason why I prefer criterion-referenced to norm-referenced tests is that criterion-referenced tests are usually specifically linked to a publicly articulated standard for good work and to curricular frameworks. This is in contrast to norm-referenced tests that claim to be "curriculum-free" or "curriculum-neutral." I don't think it makes sense to say, on the one hand, that exams are meant to hold teachers accountable and then, on the other hand, to say that there should be no link between a curriculum and a test. We should be able to look at a reading test and say, yes, indeed, this test matches the standards for good readers as described by the professional organizations of our field. We should be able to say that yes, indeed, the test values the same things that we value in our classrooms.

Too often, tests are not at all aligned with the curriculum. Let us remember Malik, the child at the start of this book who'd been making steady, slow progress in Anna's classroom and yet who scored only at the 18th percentile on his norm-referenced exam. Malik's 18th percentile score on his test—on a test we cannot see, study, learn from, or trust—is, in the end, slashed large across his teacher's proud charts of what she'd truly believed to be his progress. What is Malik supposed to believe when his teacher's values and the values on the norm-referenced tests are so contradictory? What is his teacher supposed to believe?

It is critical for us to work toward having large-scale standardized forms of assessment that are in close alignment with our standards, our curriculum frameworks, our graduate and inservice professional development, and the mission statements of our discipline-based professional organizations. There are movements afoot to design tests that do just what I have described. Perhaps the most significant of these is the New Standards project out of Pittsburgh (National Center on Education and the Economy). This project represents a national effort to recast the standards of our discipline-based professional organizations into performance measurements and to answer the questions, "How good is good enough?" and "What evidence can I look for to demonstrate what children can do?"

The New Standards assessment system has evolved out of a movement that began at the first national summit on education in 1989 when President Bush and the state governors launched a process of developing discipline-based standards. This first educational summit has been followed by others. In March 1996, forty-one governors and forty-nine chief executive officers of America's largest corporations gathered for a national education summit at which they concluded that the number one priority for schools was the adoption of international benchmark assessments. By now, disciplinary organizations (the National Council of Teachers of

English, the National Council of Teachers of Mathematics, the American Association for the Advancement of Science, and others) have all produced standards for their disciplines. Every state has also engaged in a process of developing a state-wide consensus on standards. President Clinton recently pushed this agenda even further, urging that we give students national exams in reading and mathematics based on the curriculum frameworks of the National Assessment of Educational Progress (NAEP).

The push behind the call for standards is often regarded as a conservative one. When people write and talk in support of standards, their rhetoric tends to be full of phrases like, "holding principals and teachers accountable," "clarifying expectations," "demanding mastery," and "retaining students who don't measure up." I have hesitations about the top-down, lay-down-the-law tone of this movement. Because of all this, I have been a bit wary about the push toward a standards-based curriculum. I am also aware that if schools across the nation were to adopt a criterion-referenced, standards-based assessment system, this might soon lead us toward a national curriculum and this has always, for me, been problematic because I believe that for teachers to be professionals, we need some autonomy and control, and I also believe that diversity enriches. But the truth is, despite my reservations, I'm becoming convinced that the benefits of a widely used criterion-referenced test might possibly outweigh the drawbacks. I say this for these reasons:

- I believe (or hope) such tests would be based on the goals and frameworks developed by the discipline-based organizers, and these seem to me to be light-years ahead of those embodied in most published textbooks and most school curiculums. Despite the rhetoric about top-down accountability, then, important progressive methods are being brought into schools.
- Exams that were designed to be "curriculum-free" are, in fact, already controlling curriculum. It is arguable that as long as the tests are high-stakes, they will never be curriculum-free and this then means that we should be certain we select tests that will move curriculum in a positive direction. If tests are standards-based, this means that it will be teachers and members of

professional discipline-based organizations, not publishers, who, for example, define what it means to be good readers.

- When tests are "curriculum-free," when tests are not linked to a clearly defined body of knowledge and skills, it is especially likely that some children will resign themselves to a feeling that they are doomed to do poorly on tests. Success on the test can feel out of their hands and perhaps out of their reach.

My larger belief is that although the standards movement is often fueled by a mistrust of teachers, the movement may nevertheless serve us as a teaching profession. The standards movement, and specifically the New Standards project, is proving to be something of a Trojan Horse. Under the guise of accountability and other conservative agendas, important progressive methods are being brought into schools.

We will all want to closely examine the New Standards assessment package (for more information, contact the National Center on Education and the Economy, http://www.ncee.org). Working under the direction of Marc Tucker, president of the National Center on Education and the Economy; Lauren Resnick, director of the Learning Research and Development Center at the University of Pittsburgh; and Phil Daro, executive director of New Standards, this is an impressive system. The New Standards project offers a full-assessment package that includes an on-demand criterion-based exam for fourth and eighth graders. Although these exams still include multiple-choice questions, the exams are entirely different than norm-referenced reading tests because they are open and public, and they are based on explicit standards set by teachers' organizations. The tests include components that ask students to read extended passages, and to use the information in those passages in pieces of writing. The other remarkable thing about the New Standards exams is that they are designed to stand alongside student portfolios and teacher grades, and these three sources of information are taken together in order to assess whether or not students have met the standards.

Several states, including Rhode Island and Vermont, have already adopted the New Standards exams as their state assessment measure and others are sure to do so. Meanwhile approximately thirty other states are using New Standards as a resource as they develop their own standards-based assessments.

The NAEP test, like the New Standards test, reflects a thoughtful understanding of what it means to be a good reader. This test, like the New Standards test, is truly standards based and criterion referenced. The NAEP exam, like the New Standards exam, is known for its high expectations for students. Mark Musick, head of the Southern Regional Education Board, did a comparison study of the scores earned by the same students on their state assessments with those earned on the NAEP exam (Musick, 1996). Musick found that many students scored very high on their state assessments and very low on the NAEP exam. This, of course, highlights the fact that one test's "honors" is another test's "below standard." There is no international registry of academic standards and no real clarity on what constitutes a national standard. But for now, the high standards of the NAEP and the New Standards exams offer us fairly reasonable (and high) benchmarks.

While advocating criterion-referenced exams, then, we will also want to support exams that are standards-based. Often the states develop their own pilot exams and then ask major vendors (publishers) to bring these pilot tests up to scale. The risk is that often a great deal is lost in translation. We need to speak out to be sure that once vendors develop their "standards-based" tests, they bring them back to the standards committee for approval. Currently, it is the *publisher,* not the committee, who is expected to answer the question, "Is this test standards-based?" It doesn't need to be this way. We can insist that the educators who participate in developing a consensus around certain standards be the ones to evaluate whether tests match the standards.

It is worth noticing that both the NAEP and the New Standards exams are not only standards-based and criterion-referenced, they are also *performance assessments*. That is, children are asked to demonstrate what they can do as readers by actually reading extended texts and responding to them in short essays, in short answers, and in responses to prompts and questions.

Performance-assessment exams are more costly than tests that are entirely multiple choice. Some norm-referenced tests cost just over a dollar per child, for example, and the New Standards exams cost closer to $12.00 per child. Of course, I argue that performance assessments are worth the investment. One way to limit the cost of the exams is to give them to only a very few grade levels. A second way to limit costs is to give the tests to only a sampling of the student population. For example, because the purpose of the NAEP test has been to document long-term trends in the teaching of reading, it wasn't important that each and every student take the test and earn a score on it. Therefore, the NAEP test has been given to a carefully selected, rather limited sampling of the population. This has made it possible to give this more open-ended test, one that avoids a heavy reliance on multiple-choice questions, without incurring extravagant costs. It would be wise for all of us to follow this important example. The purpose of large-scale assessment is to document and reveal trends across large groups, not to reveal details about individuals. It isn't necessary to give large-scale exams to every individual.

On the other hand, if the public requires a score for every individual, we can certainly give performance exams to all students. More and more states are including performance components in their state tests. We as teachers can feel very good about this because these improvements on large-scale exams have come about because of pressure from teachers who have insisted that reading tests must test reading. It is no accident, for example, that McGraw-Hill's newest test is called Terra Nova, meaning "new ground." The test is not as new as many of us would like, but the fact that a large vendor like McGraw-Hill is trying to offer a more performance-oriented test is a step in the right direction.

It is also important for us to remember that large-scale tests are not all equally bad. As long as reading is being tested through multiple-choice questions, we will want to agitate for reform. But there is a world of difference between, for example, the Iowa Test of Basic Skills on one extreme and the NAEP exam on the other. There is even a wide difference between the Iowa Test of Basic Skills and a norm-referenced test like the Sanford 9. Teachers need to help influence the choice of tests.

When the day comes that we have criterion-referenced, standards-based, and performance exams, these exams will help hold us on course in our teaching. The tests will never be ideal, nor will they be tailored to each of us, but they can embody and remind us of goals that the professional community deems important. While we work to achieve the goal of putting such tests into place, there are smaller, but crucial, adjustments that we as teachers will want to advocate.

Becoming Advocates for a Kinder, Fairer, and More Open System of Assessment

We must argue for a more open system of testing and of reporting of scores. In my state, teachers barely catch a glimpse of the exams that exert such control over us and our children. We unseal the exams just minutes before we distribute them, and then the instant the testing session is over, the exams are whisked off to the central office. They are never returned to us. Instead, we receive reams of paperwork detailing our students' achievements on each of twenty-some subskills. These statistical breakdowns probably cost thousands and thousands of dollars. I'm confident the money could better be spent providing books for classrooms. I have never met a teacher who trusts the computer analysis of her students' exams. For example, over and over we hear that students have difficulty with inference when those of us who know the particular student and the particular question are usually quite certain that the cause of the error was, instead, a lack of background knowledge.

The larger point, however, is that only someone who knows the student can hope to imagine the intelligence behind students' errors. Why is it we are not all able to look at our students' tests, to learn from their work? In some states (including, for example, Texas), the tests are returned to teachers after they have been scored. This should be regarded as an essential right for all of us.

The fact that we never see the tests our students take means we can't protest inadequate questions such as those I cited earlier in this book because we never get to see those questions. We can't test-prep or teach with a knowledge of last year's test. Apparently someone thinks this would give us an unfair advantage. Yet how fair is it that the publishers have access to these tests and can then proceed to write their textbooks based on this privileged knowledge? I think it is not fair when the same outfit writes both the tests and curriculum.

I do not agree with the fact that major publishers write both norm-referenced reading tests and then also write basal reading textbooks (which publishers proceed to argue are "proven methods" of teaching reading based on instances when students who follow the basals earn higher scores on the tests). I also do not approve of recent reports that the primary authors of New Standards may write an accompanying teacher's guide and curriculum.

As teachers, we must speak out for the right to study our children's tests, to learn from their errors and their successes. We should also be more assertive over our rights to see the tests themselves—both those our children will take and those given in far corners of the country. It is not difficult to write to testing vendors and receive copies of the tests (for the cost of $1.25 or $1.75 each) and it is helpful to have an array of different tests on file and to see the differences among them. This can help us realize that all tests are not created equal.

We should also ask for full disclosure of any formulas for deriving scores associated with the tests. If the newspapers have a secret formula for arriving at a school's "index of poverty" or for accounting for extenuating circumstances in a school, all of this should be open to the public. We cannot challenge the logic behind formulas that are kept shrouded.

When I say, "we should ask for full disclosure of formulas for deriving scores," I'm probably not using strong enough words. For this and for many other rights we need to do more than "ask" for things. We need to publish, lobby, argue, rally, organize, and write for these things. A friend of mine is a Washington-based lobbyist and part of her work involves trying to organize teachers to speak out on behalf of children, schools, and the education profession. "I'm so frustrated by the project of trying to organize teachers," she said to me. "Teachers constitute the largest profession on earth. Why don't they understand their power? But they won't raise their voices to speak out. Why not?" Her question is a crucial one.

When an article comes out in the papers claiming that teachers are failing to teach because 30 percent of children are below grade level, we must write and tell readers that tests are designed so that a full 50 percent of children will inevitably be below grade level. When a journalist awards gold stars to schools that earn high test scores, we must write to pull back the curtains, to reveal some of the injustices done out of a single-minded focus on improved scores.

Our voices do matter. A magazine editor will take great notice when he or she receives even just five letters in response to a story. And my Washington activist tells me that the rule of thumb in her organizational work is that it takes twenty letters for a Congressperson to take notice of an issue, and a mere sixty letters to turn that issue into a priority. Our individual voices matter, and our voices can matter especially if we gather together with others who feel as we do.

We tell young people about the power of print. "The pen is mightier than the sword," we say, and show children how Martin Luther King's "I Have A dream" speech and Abraham Lincoln's Gettysburg Address changed the course of history. Seventy percent of the people who are jailed as political prisoners, whose dissent so upsets the political systems that they are put in jail, are writers. We tell children about the power of print, but if we, as a profession, realized the power of print, the world of tests would be very different indeed.

We must write and speak out to insist that a wide range of student scores be taken into account when evaluating a school's progress. In Texas, for example, the scores of every school are disaggregated according to race, socioeconomics, and host of other variables. A school is only regarded as successful if there has been upward progress for each one of these populations as well as for the school as a whole. Educators from Texas have told me that this alone has transformed the mission of schools across the state.

We must speak out against the new trend to bring standardized, norm-referenced tests back into the primary grades. How tragic it is to see this! When I first met Ted Chittenden, he told me that there has been some progress in the last decade of assessment work, as demonstrated by the fact that multiple-choice, norm-referenced tests were no longer in the primary grades. Now, alas, all that progress is being lost. We can and must write to express outrage.

We need to speak out often about students' rights to equitable "opportunities to learn." This should be happening across the nation. One of the great ironies of large-scale assessments is that although people claim their primary purpose is to hold people accountable to ensuring that all children are given equal opportunities to learn, the single, clearest conclusion one can draw from the tests is that children in different towns and cities, children of different racial and socioeconomic groups, are *not* all achieving similarly. And it is clear that at least some (and probably most) of the reason for this is that children are not given equal opportunities to learn. In at least one state, people have sued over this issue. They asked, How can all our children be expected to achieve comparably on one test when the opportunities for children to learn are not equal? As a result of the court case, schools in the state's poorest areas were given more resources. We know that access to books, for example, is crucial to students' achievements on reading tests (McQuillan, 1998). If we are going to argue for equal opportunities to learn, we need to argue for equal classroom libraries. At present, some children have very little access to books, others have tremendous access. The inequities from children's homes are matched by parallel inequities in their classrooms.

Finally and perhaps most importantly, we as teachers need to go the ends of the earth to be sure that our assessment practices do not interfere with our goals of supporting our students' learning. In order to do this we need to keep in mind that standardized large-scale tests are instruments designed to show large-scale trends in student achievement. These large-scale assessments are not the fine-tuned, responsive assessment tools that one might use to make a decision about any one particular child's progress.

One of the most important principles of the National Forum on Assessment is that "important decisions about individuals, such as program placement, grade promotions, or graduation must not be made on the basis of any single assessment," (*National Forum Assessment Systems*, 1995, p.8). Ted Chittenden and Jacqueline Jones from ETS speak passionately about the importance of this principle. This is significant because their outfit makes the tests and yet they do not want the tests to ever be used except in concert with multiple forms of evidence. Ted and Jacqueline say it is their knowledge of tests that makes it so clear that tests must be just one variable that we consider in our decisions about children. Decisions about individual children are best made by teachers and other school staff based on frequent and regular classroom assessments.

Developing Systems for Classroom Assessment

If we raise our voices and cast our votes toward having criterion-referenced, standards-based, performance-assessment exams in our districts and in our states, then as part of our effort to give all children the chance to work hard in school and to do well on the clearly delineated expectations, we'll want to specify goals for classroom work and give children and their parents clear and frequent indicators of their progress toward these goals. Teachers across a single grade level, for example, in a school or district might develop a consensus about the number and the difficulty level of books we hope students at that grade-level will be able to read with proficiency. One of the most famous requirements of the New Standards assessment system, for example, is the fact that fourth graders are expected to need twenty-five books (or the equivalent) at the level we see in books like *Matilda* or *Ramona*. Other assessment systems, including the *Primary Language Record*, New York State Elementary Literacy Profile (Falk, 1998), and First Steps, are less intent on delineating expected levels and more focused on giving us, as teachers, accurate and compelling descriptions of the stages of development based on performance indicators. This way, we can describe where a child is and where the child needs to go next. It is crucially important that these classroom-based assessment systems exist and that they are linked to the large-scale assessments so that classroom-based, day-to-day assessment provides concrete ways to support each child's progress toward goals the district has deemed significant.

The problem is that when our states continue to measure students and teachers by norm-referenced, multiple-choice tests—that do not seem to us to really be testing reading at all—it's impossible to have a clearly articulated relationship between classroom-based record keeping and the tests. A problematic consequence is that often, as a result, we end up teaching without the benefit of clear goals. That is, I worry that our current assessment system can actually lure us away from teaching toward clear goals. The tragedy of norm-referenced reading tests is that too often they sit on the horizon of our teaching, clouding out any other goals, any other images of what it is we are aiming toward in our teaching. When we and our children are judged by one thing only—their scores on norm-referenced reading tests—and yet those tests aren't designed to direct our teaching, what the reading tests do is undermine and call into question all the other directions and goals we have, leaving our teaching rudderless and fraught with ambivalence. The great irony of these reading tests is that although they are supposedly an effort to hold teachers accountable, to keep us hooked into the absolute need to move children along as readers, writers, and learners, the tests accomplish just the opposite. The other day, I was with a progressive teacher, a woman who attends many professional conferences and tries to bring everything she learns back to her classroom. Her children are in reading partnerships, writing response groups, book clubs, author studies—the works. Yet watching her, it seemed that something big was missing from her teaching. As her children worked on activities related to a Leo Leoni author study, I tried to put my finger on why her children seemed disengaged and off-handed about their work. They were all doing something, but I couldn't quite see what the various activities were leading toward or what skills and aptitudes were being developed. Looking for the purpose and the direction behind the class's activities, I asked the teacher, "Why did you choose to do this author study?"

The woman looked at me, as if bewildered by the question. "Why an author study?" she repeated, unsure she'd heard me right. Didn't I know that author studies were good things? "Why? I don't know why. Why not?" Then she added, "It was something to do. And we had the books."

Searching for another way to discern her purpose, I asked, "How will you know when you are done?"

"When we get sick of it," she answered.

I've been haunted by this conversation. It rides my consciousness because I think this is the great trap of norm-referenced "curriculum-free" reading tests. I suspect the teacher with her Leo Lionni study didn't have clear, observable goals for her author study in part because she has been given the message that the tests are all that count. Yet those tests have no direct link to her class-room. She test-preps toward the goal of higher tests scores, but given that no one has helped her to really articulate her goals for her children as readers, she seems to teach toward the goal of an engaged, happy, productive feeling in the classroom. Conse-quently her teaching has become all about neat things to do to keep her kids somewhat productive. When this is our goal, we, as teachers, have lost our ability to be regenerated and held on course by feedback from our children's progress or lack of progress.

The goal can't be to fill time, or even to have a well-managed, productive aura in our classrooms. The goal must be to grow avid, capable readers, writers, learners. The goal must be to make each of our children smart.

For school to be a place where Malik becomes smart, two things are essential in any assessment system that is going to give Anna, Malik, and the rest of us feedback on Malik's progress. First, prob-ably Malik and certainly Malik's teacher need to be clear about where Malik stands in comparison to fourth graders across the globe. Obviously it is reasonable for some standardized measure to exist that can point out that despite Malik's progress, he still has a ways to go. Secondly, Malik needs to know what exactly is expected of him so he can progress toward those clearly spelled-out goals. Ideally, the goals that his teacher articulates and charts his progress toward will be totally aligned to the goals against which Malik is judged on test day.

But often times, we teach and live in an imperfect world. For now our children will often have to take tests that are not aligned to our curriculum and to our beliefs. What are we to do?

When I was young I spent several weeks of each summer at a camp. Always, on the last night, we'd gather at dusk at the edge of a lake. We'd each bring a block of wood carved into the shape of a boat, and each boat held a candle. For the final ritual before we dis-persed to our homes, each one of us would light our candle, and then set it afloat on the lake. As our candles bobbed and drifted into the dark corners of the lake, we'd stand, arms linked, singing "This little light of mine, I'm going to let it shine. . . ."

It can be dark out there in the world of teaching, What are we to do?

I want to remember the lessons from Camp Aloha. I want to remember that my charge, my responsibility, is to let my flicker of candlelight shine. "Hide it under a bushel, no, I'm going to let it shine." I can make a difference just by letting Jasmine know that her 71 score is not the final judgment on who she is as a reader and as a human being. I can make a difference by remembering that test preparation need not feel like test day itself. I can make a difference by telling the untold stories that hide in the corners and columns of score sheets. And perhaps above all, I can make a difference by remembering that on that final night at Camp Aloha, all of us campers linked arms together.

In the schools I know best throughout New York City, staff room conversations are changing. Teachers are less apt to sit clustered, with each cluster at the opposite ends of a long table. More and more we're pulling together to talk. We are talking about assessment. We're asking, "What is it we hope our children will be able to do as readers? As writers? What evidence will we look for to show us that they are on track?" The tests are still there, of course, but we're finding that the tests lose a little bit of their power when we, as a profession, reach out for the tools to conduct our assessments sitting side by side with children.

National Center for Fair & Open Testing (Fair Test),
342 Broadway, Cambridge, MA 02139, email: fairtest@aol.com,
website: http://www.fairtest.org

Glossary

Accountability: The process by which school districts and states attempt to ensure that schools and school systems meet their goals.

Aggregating scores: Combining the scores of individual test takers to view performance trends across groups.

Bias: A lack of objectivity, fairness, or impartiality on the part of the assessment instrument that leads to misinterpretation of student performance or knowledge.

Criterion-referenced test: Test that provides information about test takers' performance relative to a set of criteria. Test items are selected and scored to demonstrate test takers' proficiencies in relation to the criteria.

High stakes: Consequences attached to test performance such as school graduation, retention in grade, referral to special education for students, monetary and/or professional sanctions, and rewards for teachers, principals, and schools.

Norming group: A sample of test takers who represent those for whom a test is constructed. The sample should represent the different geographic, socioeconomic, racial/ethnic, and linguistic backgrounds of the test taker population in the nation.

Norm-referenced test: Test that provides information about how test takers' performance compares to the performance of a representative national sample of the test takers. Test items are selected and scored to demonstrate test takers' proficiencies in relation to each other.

Percentage: The score in relation to the total points possible. For example, if a test taker scored 7 points out of 10, the percentage correct would be 70 percent.

Percentile: A test taker's standing in relation to others. For example, if a test taker scored 5 points out of 10 and 50 percent of those who took the test achieved above that score and below that score, the test taker would be in the 50th percentile.

Performance assessment: A way for students to demonstrate what they know and can do by applying their knowledge and skills in tasks that require them to construct their own responses, create their own products, or perform demonstrations such as writing essays, completing science experiments, solving mathematical problems, and so on.

Quartiles: The division of percentiles into four segments: the bottom quartile: 0–25th percentile; the second quartile: 25–50th percentile; the third quartile: 50–75th percentile; and the upper quartile: 75–100th percentile.

Raw scores: The number of points a test taker achieves on a test. For example, if a test taker scored 7 points out of 10, the raw score would be 7.

Reliability: The degree to which an assessment measures what it is supposed to measure consistently over time and across raters.

Standardized test: A set of predetermined questions and/or tasks administered in a uniform manner to all who take it.

Standards: Publicly-articulated expectations against which progress can be measured. The expectations can be expressed as content standards: what students should be able to know and do in different discipline areas; as performance standards: how well students are able to demonstrate their achievement of the content standards; or as opportunity-to-learn standards: the degree to which schools, districts, and/or states provide students with access to the content standards so that they can achieve the performance standards.

Standards-based test: A test that provides information about test takers' proficiencies in relation to a set of publicly articulated standards.

Stanine: A way of distributing the total points scored on a test into bands that reflect nine levels of performance.

Validity: The extent to which an assessment measures what it is supposed to measure.

Suggested Readings

Suggested Background Readings

Andrias, J., Kanevsky, R., Strieb, L.Y., & Traugh, C. (1992). *Exploring values and standards: Implications for assessment.* New York: National Center for Restructuring Education, Schools, and Teaching, (NCREST).

Baron, J.B., & Wolf, D.P. (1996). *Performance-based student assessment: Challenges and possibilities.* Chicago: National Society for the Study of Education.

Darling-Hammond, L. (1993). *Standards of practice for learner-centered schools.* New York: NCREST.

Darling-Hammond, L. (1994a). *National standards and assessments: Will they improve education?* New York: NCREST.

Darling-Hammond, L. (1994b). Performance-based assessment and educational equity. Cambridge: *Harvard Educational Review, 54* (1), 5–30.

Darling-Hammond, L., Ancess, J., & Falk, B. (1995). *Authentic assessment in action.* New York: Teachers College Press.

Edelsky, C. (1991). *With literacy and justice for all.* New York: Falmer Press.

Falk, B., (Ed.) (1994). *The Educational Forum, 59* (1) (Issue on authentic assessment).

Goodman, K. (1992). Myths, metaphors, and misuses. In K. Goodman, L. Bridges Bird, and Y. Goodman (Eds.), *The Whole Language Catalog: Supplement on Authentic Assessment.* New York, NY: SRA/Macmillan-McGraw-Hill.

Goodwin, A. (1997). Assessment for equity and inclusion: Embracing all our children. New York: Teachers College Press.

Herman, J., Aschbacher, P., & Winters, L. (1992). *A practical guide to alternative assessment.* Alexandria, VA: Association for Supervision and Curriculum Development.

Hill, C. (1992). *Testing and assessment: An ecological approach.* New York: Teachers College Press.

Kornhaber, M., & Gardner, H. (1993). *Varieties of excellence: Identifying and assessing children's talents.* New York: NCREST.

Mitchell, R. (1992). *Testing for learning: How new approaches to evaluation can improve American schools.* New York: The Free Press.

National Forum on Assessment. (1995). *Principles and indicators for student assessment systems.* Cambridge: National Center for Fair and Open Testing (FairTest).

Perrone, V. (Ed.). (1991). *Expanding student assessment.* Alexandria, VA: ASCD.

Price, J., Schwabacher, S., & Chittenden, T. (1993). *The multiple forms of evidence study.* New York: NCREST.

Rothman, R. (1993). *Measuring up: Standards, assessment, and school reform.* San Francisco: Jossey-Bass.

Shepard, L. (February, 1995). Using assessment to improve learning. *Educational Leadership*, 38–43.

Tierney, R., Carter, M., & Desai, L. (1991). *Portfolio assessment in the reading-writing classroom.* Norwood, MA: Christopher Gordon.

Valencia, S., Hiebert, E., & Afflerbach, P. (1994). *Authentic reading assessment: Practices and possibilities.* Newark, DE: International Reading Association.

Wiggins, G. (1993). *Assessing student performance: Exploring the purpose and limits of testing.* San Francisco: Jossey-Bass.

Suggested Classroom-Based Literacy Asssessment Systems

Barrs, M., Ellis, S., Hester, H., & Thomas, A. (1989). *The primary language record.* Portsmouth, NH: Heinemann.

Education Department of Western Australia. (1994). *First steps: Developmental curriculums.* Melbourne, Australia: Heinemann.

Educators in Connecticut's Pomperaug Regional School District 15. (1996). *A teacher's guide to performance-based learning and assessment.* Alexandria, VA: Association for Supervision and Curriculum Development.

Falk, B., et al. (1998). *The elementary literacy profile.* New York: NCREST.

Griffin, P., Smth, P., & Burrill, L. (1995). *The American literacy profile scales.* Portsmouth, NH: Heinemann.

Harp, B. (1996). *The handbook of literacy assessment and evaluation.* Norwood, MA: Christopher Gordon.

National Center on Education and the Economy and the University of Pittsburgh. (1997). *The new standards reference exams.* New York: Harcourt Brace.

Children's Literature

Clifton, L. (1992). *The three wishes.* New York: Dell.

Cohen, M. (1980). *First grade takes a test.* New York: Greenwillow.

Dahl, R. (1964). *Charlie and the chocolate factory.* New York: Knopf.

Lewis, C. S. (1950). *The chronicles of Narnia.* New York: Macmillan.

Lobel, A. (1971). *Frog and toad.* New York: HarperCollins.

Lowry, L. (1993). *The giver.* New York: Bantam Doubleday Dell.

MacLachlan, P. (1985). *Sarah, plain and tall.* New York: Harper Collins.

Myers, W. D. (1994). *The glory field.* New York: Scholastic.

Naylor, P. R. (1991). *Shiloh.* New York: Dell.

Pullman, P. (1995). *The golden compass.* New York: Knopf.

Reynolds, J. (1980). *Stone fox.* New York: Harper and Row.

Taylor, T. (1992). *The cay.* New York: Doubleday.

Warner, G. C. (1942). *Boxcar children.* Morton Grove, IL: Albert Whitman.

White, E. B. (1952). *Charlotte's web.* New York: Harper and Row.

Wilder, L. I. (1935). *Little house on the prairie.* New York: Harper and Row.

Wynne-Jones, T. (1995). *The maestro.* New York: Orchard Books.

Yolen, J. (1987). *Owl moon.* New York: Philomel.

Zillions magazine. New York: Consumers Union of U.S.

References

Adams, M. (1990). *Beginning to Read: Thinking and learning about print.* Cambridge, MA: The MIT Press.

Anderson, R., Wilson, P., & Fielding, L. (1988). Growth in reading and how children spend their time outside of school. *Reading Research Quarterly, 23,* 285–303.

Barr, M. (1998). *The Learning Record. Handbook for Teachers, K–6,* with Margaret Syverson; and *Handbook for Teachers, 6–12.* Portsmouth, NH: Heinemann.

Berliner, D.C., & Biddle, B. (1995). *The manufactured crisis: Myths, fraud, and the attack on America's public schools.* Reading, MA: Addison-Wesley.

Boyer, E. (1983). *High school.* New York: Harper & Row.

Bracey, G. (1997). *The truth about American schools: the Bracey reports 1991–97.* Bloomington, IN: Phi Delta Kappan Educational Foundation.

Cannell, J.J. (1987). *Nationally normed elementary achievement testing in America's public schools: How all fifty states are above the national average.* Daniels, WV: Friends for Education.

Cannell, J.J. (1989). *How public educators cheat on standardized achievement tests.* Albuquerque, NM: Friends for Education.

Chall, J. (1967/1983). *Learning to read: The great debate.* New York: McGraw-Hill.

Collins, J. (1997, October 27). How Johnny should read. *Time,* 78–81.

Darling-Hammond, L. (1989). Curiouser and curiouser: Alice in testingland. *Rethinking Schools 3*(2), 1, 17.

Darling-Hammond, L. (1990). Achieving our goals: Superficial or structural reforms? *Phi Delta Kappan 72*(4), 286–295.

Darling-Hammond, L. (1991). The implications of testing policy for educational quality and equality. *Phi Delta Kappan 73*(3), 220–225.

Darling-Hammond, L. (1994). Performance-based assessment and educational equity. *Harvard Educational Review 64,* 5–30.

Darling-Hammond, L. (1997). *The Right to learn.* San Francisco: Jossey-Bass.

Darling-Hammond, L., & Wise, A. (1985). Beyond standardization: State standards and school improvement. *The Elementary School Journal 85*(3), 315–336.

Edelsky, C. (1991). *With literacy and justice for all.* New York: Falmer Press.

Education Week. (1997, January 15). Comparing test results. Online: http://www. eduweek. org.

Elley, W. (1994). Preface. In W. Elley (Ed.), *The IEA study of reading literacy: Achievement and instruction in thirty-two school systems* (pp. xxi–xxii). Oxford: Pergamon.

Elley, W. (1996). Lifting literacy levels in developing countries: Some implications from an IEA study. In V. Greaney (Ed.), *Promoting reading in developing countries: Views on making reading materials accessible to increase literacy levels* (pp. 39–54). Newark, DE: International Reading Association.

Falk, B., et al. (1998). The elementary literacy profile. New York: National Center for Restructuring Education, Schools, and Teaching (NCREST).

Fair Test. (nd). K-12 testing: Fact sheet. Based on Fair Test's comprehensive study *Fallout from the testing explosion,* N. Medina and M. Neill. Cambridge, MA: National Center for Fair and Open Testing.

Feldman, S. (1998). Report card: How the city's third graders measured up: *New York Times.* March 8, 1998. Section 14, 10–11.

Flower, L., & Hayes, J.R. (1980). The dynamics of composing: Making plans and juggling constraints. In L. Gregg and E. Steinberg (Eds.), *Cognitive processes in writing.* Hillsdale, NJ: Lawrence Erlbaum Associates.

Goodlad, J. (1984). *A place called school: Prospects for the future.* New York: McGraw-Hill.

Goodman, K. (1992). Myths, metaphors, and misuses. In K. Goodman, L. Bridges Bird, and Y. Goodman (Eds.), *The whole language catalog: Supplement on authentic assessment.* New York: SRA/Macmillan-McGraw-Hill.

Hanania, J. (1995, May 28). Sinking scores? Not in the numbers. *Los Angeles Times.*

Haney, W., & Madaus, G. (1986). Effects of standardized testing and the future of the National Assessment of Educational Progress. Working paper for the NAEP study group. Chestnut Hill, MA: Center for the Study of Testing, Evaluation, and Educational Policy.

Hanson, F.A. (1993). *Testing testing.* Berkeley: University of California Press.

Harman, S. (1996). New life for old tests. *In Thrust for Educational Leadership.* May/June, 20–23.

Hill, C. (1992). Testing and assessment: An ecological approach. New York: Teachers College Press.

Jones, K. & Whitford, B. (1997, December). Kentucky's conflicting reform principles. *Phi Delta Kappan, 79*(4).

Kantrowitz, B., & Wingert, P. (1989, April 17). How kids learn. *Newsweek*, 50–57.

Katzman, J., & Hodas, S. (1995). *Class action: How to create accountability, innovation, and excellence in American schools.* New York: Villard.

Kibby, M. (1995). *Student literacy: Myths and realities.* Bloomington, IN: Phi Delta Kappan Educational Foundation.

Koretz, D. (1988). Arriving in Lake Wobegon: Are standardized tests exaggerating achievement and distorting instruction? *American Educator* 12(2), 8–15, 46–52.

Krashen, S. (1996). *Every person a reader: An alternative to the California Task Force Report on Reading.* Culver City, CA: Language Education Associates.

Krashen, S. (1997). When whole language means real reading it does well in method comparison studies. Manuscript submitted for publication.

Lemann, N. (1997, November) The reading wars. *Atlantic Monthly*, 128–134.

Manning, G., Manning, M., & Long, R., (1989). Effects of a whole language and a skills-oriented program on the literacy development of inner city primary children. ERIC: ED 324 642

McKnight, C.C., Crosswhite, F.J., Dossey, J.A., Kifer, E., Swafford, S.O., Travers, K.J., & Cooney, F. J. (1987). *The underachieving curriculum: Assessing U.S. school mathematics from an international perspective.* Champaign, IL: Stipes Publishing.

McQuillan, J. (1988). *The literacy risis: False claims, real solutions.* Portsmouth, NH: Heinemann.

Meier, D. (1991, Fall). Why the reading tests don't test reading. *Dissent*, 457–466.

Moustafa, M. (1997). *Beyond traditional phonics: Research discoveries and reading instruction.* Portsmouth, NH: Heinemann.

Mullis, Campbell, and Farstrup. (1993). *Executive summary of the NAEP 1992 reading report card for the nation and the states.* Washington, D.C.: U.S. Department of Education.

Musick, Mark. (1996). *Setting education standards high enough.* Atlanta, GA: Southern Regional Education Board.

National Assessment for Educational Progress. (1981). *Reading, thinking, and writing: Results from the 1979–1980 national assessment of reading and literature.* Denver, CO: NAEP.

National Association for the Education of Young Children. (1988). NAEYC position statement on developmentally appropriate practice in the primary grades, serving five- through eight-year-olds. *Young Children* 43(2), 64–84.

National Center for Fair and Open Testing. (1995). *Principles and indicators for student assessment systems.* Cambridge, MA.

National Center on Education and the Economy. (1997). *Elementary school performance standards, Volume 1, New Standards.* Pittsburgh, PA.

Popham, J. (1991, Winter). Appropriateness of teachers' test preparation practices. *Educational Measurement: Issues and Practice,* 12–15.

Rothman, R. (1995). *Measuring up: Standards, assessment, and school reform.* San Francisco: Jossey-Bass.

Shaughnessy, M. (1977). *Errors and expectations.* New York: Oxford University Press.

Shepard, L. (1989). *Inflated test score gains: Is it old norms or teaching to the test?* Los Angeles: Center for the Study of Evaluation, UCLA.

Slavin, R.E. (1997). Can education reduce social inequity? *Educational Leadership, 55*(4).

Trelease, J. (1995). *The read-aloud handbook.* (Rev. ed.) New York: Penguin.

Tucker, Marc S., & Codding, Judy B. (1998). *Standards for our schools.* San Francisco: Jossey–Bass.

Weaver, C., Gillmeister-Krause, L., & Vento-Zogby, G. (1996). *Creating support for effective literacy education.* Portsmouth, NH: Heinemann.

Webster, R., McInnis, E., & Crover, L. (1986). Curriculum biasing effects in standardized and criterion-referenced reading achievement tests. *Psychology in the Schools, 23,* 205–213.

Wiggins, G. (1993). *Assessing student performance: Exploring the purpose and limits of testing.* San Francisco: Jossey-Bass.

Index